CHILDREN AS STO[...]

Children as Storytellers

Kerry Mallan

Primary English Teaching Association
NSW, Australia

Heinemann
Portsmouth, New Hampshire

Heinemann
A division of Reed Elsevier Inc.
361 Hanover Street Portsmouth, NH 03801-3912
Offices and agents throughout the world

©1991 Primary English Teaching Association
Laura St, Newtown NSW 2042 Australia

First U.S. Printing 1992

Acknowledgments

The author wishes to acknowledge the various people who helped make this book a reality. My thanks to:

- the children and teachers of Moorooka State School and Kruger State School, for their participation, enthusiasm and friendship;

- Meg Philp Paterson, for steering me in this direction and for the inspiration of her pioneering work in storytelling;

- my family, for their wonderful stories — especially my parents, who were my first storytellers;

- my friends and colleagues, for sharing insights and offering calm reassurance during my many moments of frustration and self-doubt.

And special thanks to Mick, whose patience, critical judgment and support helped me to keep on the task and not give up.

Library of Congress Cataloging-in-Publication Data

Mallan, Kerry.
  Children as storytellers / Kerry Mallan.
    p. cm.
  Reprint. Originally published: Newtown, NSW, Australia : Primary
English Teaching Association. 1991.
  Includes bibliographical references (p.).
  ISBN 0-435-08779-7 (U.S.)
  1. Storytelling Study and teaching   2. Language arts.
  I. Title.
  LB1042.M256 1992
  808.5' 43 — dc20   92-20527
                                                                        CIP

Photographs: Mick Mallan
Cover design: Judi Pownall
Cover artwork: Students of Rozelle Public School, NSW
Editor: Deborah Brown
Typeset in 11/12pt Palatino by Adtype Graphics

Printed in the United States of America on Acid Free Paper
94 95 96   9 8 7 6 5 4 3 2

CONTENTS

BEGINNINGS

A story. A story.
Let it come. Let it go.

African ritual opening

Childhood is a time full of stories. Those of us who were fortunate enough to live in households where stories were told as a matter of course have grown into our adult years with a rich endowment. These family stories, anecdotes and reminiscences are meant to be passed on, embellished and shared with the people we love. Stories grow from stories and so we keep adding to our inheritance every day of our lives.

The stories I remember from my childhood came not so much from printed texts, though I was given books for birthdays and at Christmas time, but more from the stories that my parents told me. My father filled my head with wonderful stories of his English schooldays in a strict Catholic boarding school; of the harsh punishment meted out when he was caught smoking in the toilets — having to kneel all night before a holy statue on a cold, hard chapel floor. The punishment proved an ineffectual deterrent, for my father and his accomplices nearly burnt down the school in a later encounter with the illicit pleasures of nicotine.

These stories told of the darker side of life, like the fairytales of Grimm and the stories of Dickens. They were not insipid, but full-bodied stories; they were also told with humour. Perhaps the humour made them palatable — and, after all, my father had obviously survived!

There were other stories: my parents' first meeting on a hot, dusty road in Singapore just after the Second World War; the time my mother as a young woman attended a thirty-six course banquet at a sultan's palace in Johore; our dog Spot, who thought he was a cat and liked to sleep on a neighbour's fence; my brother, aged 4, singing 'Danny Boy' at a wedding reception with all the imitated sincerity and style of Al Jolson; my mother's terror on awakening to see a huge rat above her in the mosquito net; and her unforgettable experience when, as a young child, she was forced to kiss her dead great-aunt, lying in her coffin. It seemed like the stuff that movies were made of — but these stories were real. There was one exception; a rather fanciful story which made me believe I was of royal blood. I proceeded to tell my Grade 4 classmates and teacher that I was really an Irish

1

princess. Though my teacher told me to check the authenticity of my claim, and my classmates half-believed and half-mocked me, I continued to believe and enjoy my tale for what it was. It gave me a special feeling of magic and make-believe.

Family get-togethers were another rich source of stories. At such gatherings I could listen to all the stories of times past and laugh as the funny side of our lives was recalled. They were happy times. I was not always the listener; I often had an attentive audience for the stories, jokes and exaggerated tales that I wanted to share with my extended family and friends. No one person was given the role of storyteller, for it was just accepted that every one of us had stories to share.

Though my father and other members of my family have gone, the stories they told me over the years have stayed with me. The stories yet to be told will also become an important part of my life. Now I tell stories of our family history — of times past and present. My husband brings his own stories of a very different childhood. Together our stories and the stories our children share with us are expanding our view of the world and creating tapestries of our lives and who we are.

My family is not unique in its oral tradition. Stories — about everyday life, people, places visited, special occasions — are there in every family. It is sad when families do not give life to these stories, but bury them in long-forgotten memories. In cultures where the storytellers have died without passing on their stories, there has been an irretrievable loss of a cultural heritage. The same is true for our times.

The oral tradition is important for schools as well as families. Storytelling provides a way for children and teachers to engage in creative and imaginative learning.

Teachers, for as long as there have been teachers, have taught using story. The power of children's imagination as an intellectual force for learning has not always enjoyed the same degree of academic research and respectability as more tangible outcomes of cognitive ability. According to Bruner (in Rosen, B. 1988, p. 169), narrative is an important mode of thought which helps us to order our experiences and construct reality. Unless children's ability to use narrative in their thinking, speaking and writing is given the same degree of time and attention as analytical thought, then we are failing as teachers in our responsibility to allow our students to develop the full range of their cognitive ability.

The emphasis on literature in language arts programs has given written texts prominence in primary classrooms. Today's children are perhaps better read, and read to more, than previous generations. Yet oral stories tend to be neglected. Teachers and children have their own treasure-chests of stories to be unlocked and shared. Harold Rosen (in Rosen, B. 1988, p. 167) states the case for storytelling in schools most fervently:

. . . we have been so mesmerised by the intellectual culture of our times, so intimidated by spurious claims for the superiority of what has come to be called 'expository discourse', that we are frequently disposed to be apologetic about narrative.

While the written narrative is seen as important for the reading, writing and listening aspects of the language arts, the oral narrative — through storytelling — lags behind.

This book explores ways for teachers to give children the opportunity to create and retell oral stories; not just for their entertainment value, but more importantly as a way of making sense of experiences encountered both within and outside the classroom. The teacher must be committed to storytelling, but instead of assuming the role of 'wise elder' must allow children the right to tell stories as well. The sharing of stories between adult and child is the basis for forming a relationship. Just as we come to know members of our own families by sharing our life experiences, so too can teachers and children come to know each other better through these exchanges.

The following chapters examine the place of storytelling in schools. While the emphasis is on children as storytellers, teachers will need to model and share stories and reveal themselves as people in order to establish an open climate. Through storytelling, children stand to gain academically, socially and personally: a fact that is supported by a growing body of research, both in Australia and overseas. I have attempted to incorporate much of this research and to offer practical suggestions for implementing the ideas.

Chapter 1

WHAT IS STORYTELLING?

Tell me the story about when you were a little
girl and a lady phoned to tell you that your dog
Spot was watching TV in her lounge room.

Kimberley, aged 8

Storytelling is so basic to human existence that we often cannot see that we all engage in telling some form of story every day of our lives. Some individuals have a special gift for telling stories to an enraptured audience, but we are all capable of being storytellers. Storytelling is defined most simply as using oral language in a social context to relate something heard, read, witnessed, dreamt or experienced. Peck (1989, p. 138) offers another definition: 'Storytelling is the oral interpretation of a traditional, literary, or personal experience story'.

Storytelling and storyreading

Storytelling is different from storyreading, though the two are often confused. Storytelling is born out of the oral tradition; storyreading depends on the written text. Both are important ways of sharing stories. The important difference between storytelling and storyreading lies in the interaction that occurs between teller and audience. With storytelling, the interaction is creative, as both teller and listener create the story. Words are used to create mental pictures of the story. The storyteller's face, voice, body and personality help to convey meaning and mood.

During storyreading both listener and reader are conscious of the book. With a picture book, the audience focuses on the illustrations to help their appreciation and understanding of the story. There is occasional eye contact between reader and listeners and this helps to make the connection between them.

In storytelling the sharing of the story is more personal, in that the storyteller connects more directly with the audience through eyes, gesture, voice and proximity. The teller is also free to use his or her own words within the framework of the story. Freedom of language and of movement add to the personal nature of storytelling. The storyteller learns to work not only with the language of the story but also with its structures so that changes, adjustments and emphases can be made in response to the audience's reactions.

According to Livo and Rietz (1986, p. 7), storytelling 'has a historic, ritual, rule-governed, patterned integrity'. Storytelling is an ancient art form. All previous generations used storytelling as part of their daily survival and entertainment and to preserve their cultural identity and history. Storytelling uses rituals, rules and patterns in its performance. There is a long-established expectation that a story session will proceed according to a pattern: ritual openings and endings, the degree of formality adopted by the teller, the willing transition by audience and teller from the primary world of the present to the secondary world of story, the form of audience participation in the story, the setting — all form part of the storytelling experience.

Traditional and personal story sources

Traditional literature has its origins in the oral stories, songs, myths, legends, dances and religious ceremonies of the earliest people. These stories tell of the human condition, and their appeal today lies in our ability to see ourselves in these old tales. Jane Yolen (1981, p. 15) has referred to folklore as 'a living fossil that refuses to die'. The archaeological analogy fits, for layers of civilisations become exposed as each story is shared. Many of the traditional stories we tell today have been written down, but they still need the human voice to give them colour and power and to restore them to their original oral state.

Today's 'myths' are made by films, current affairs shows, rock music, talkback shows, newspaper articles and so on, all of which add to the stories of modern civilisation. This book focuses on traditional stories and stories from our personal lives as sources for using storytelling with children. Very little emphasis has been given to contemporary fiction, for a number of reasons. The most important of these is that if children are to develop confidence and competence in their own storytelling abilities, then it is easier for them to begin with their own personal stories and the stories of folktales which have recognisable story structures, repeated language patterns and familiar motifs, characters, settings and themes. As for picture books, they make storytelling (as opposed to storyreading) very difficult because the illustrations are often an integral part of the work; to tell the story without the illustrations does it an injustice. Picture books are better read so that they can be enjoyed as a celebration of text and illustrations.

The emphasis of this book is the oral sharing of stories for the enhancement of speaking and listening skills. Reading and writing are seen by this author as important spin-offs from storytelling. Through storytelling, children will come to the printed text with a degree of familiarity and certain expectations of story structure, language and patterns.

Chapter 2

WHY CHILDREN AS STORYTELLERS?

'From this day and going on forever', proclaimed the Sky God, 'my stories belong to Ananse and shall be called "Spider Stories".'

A Story, a Story (Haley 1972)

Since the beginning of humankind, stories have been told to inform, to entertain and to explain. Traditionally, the role of the storyteller has been ascribed to an adult. The wise elder of the tribe explains the phenomena of nature and tribal lore to the younger members. Japan's kamishibai street entertainer tells stories to children and adults who gather round his theatre. Parents tell their children family stories which have been passed on from one generation to the next. The teacher uses story in all its forms to instruct the class. Children, too, have always been storytellers, but without receiving the same status or recognition as their adult counterparts. Children need to tell stories and make them their own so that, like Ananse, they will have stories named after them. In schools, both in Australia and overseas, the attention is shifting from the teacher as storyteller to the child as storyteller; a shift which springs from a sound background in language learning theory. This chapter, drawing on research published over the past decade, has as its kernel the part that storytelling plays in developing children's oracy skills. I have attempted to explore this kernel and the surrounding husks in order to highlight the positive rewards that can be won for children when we formally guide them into the role of storyteller.

Imagination

Children have robust imaginations. In spite of external attempts to curb their powers of imagination, children will continue to play in fantasy worlds, for imagination is controlled from within. This phenomenon was

9

described by Chukovsky (1963) in his book *From Two to Five*, which examined how a Russian child, denied his rich heritage of fairytales, was able to let fantasy re-emerge in his day-to-day play and conversation. We can lead children into imagining and creating, but the extent of our endeavours will never be fully apparent, at least to us and other observers. Through storytelling children can use their imaginations to visualise characters, settings and details of the action. Such is the power of story that the imagination is challenged to admit new possibilities and refashion old conceptions. The traditional story 'In a Dark, Dark Wood' (Ferguson & Durkin 1989) provides an excellent example of how visualisation occurs as a personal response. Both listeners and teller can engage in a range of different imaginings with each scene in the story: woods, house, staircase, door, room . . . After having this story told to them, a group of 12-year-old children were asked to draw what they imagined the woods were like. They described very personal and different settings (see figure 2.1). Similarly, the drawings of the 'house' were different in terms of how each listener imagined it (see figure 2.2).

Before the surprise climax in this story is revealed, listeners take part in a kind of predictive play, anticipating — perhaps wishing for — a scary outcome. Depending on the ending chosen by the storyteller (e.g. 'a mouse' or 'a ghost'), the listeners may be pleased to have their prediction confirmed; or surprised and amused that they were somehow tricked into believing that the mystery ending would involve something more terrifying than a mouse. The sense of audience and that particular moment of telling combine to give the storyteller the cue as to which ending to choose. Children can learn to respond to their particular audience, to the mood they have created, and to exercise that power of the storyteller to confirm their audience's expectations or to surprise them. Crosson and Stailey (1988, p. 8) believe that there is nothing 'preconceived' about storytelling, unlike television. They say that through storytelling, 'children will be actively participating in the story and not just receiving another programmed version of the Saturday morning television variety'.

The importance of developing children's imaginations cannot be stressed too much in today's rapidly changing, high-tech world. Exercising their imaginations is an important stage in the development of higher level thinking skills. Young children are actively encouraged to use their imaginations in play and talk, but as they grow older the adult world tends to dismiss these 'flights of fancy' as immature. Yet all people need to nurture their imaginations and let them soar in fantastic flight. Many of the inventions of the modern world might not have been conceived had someone not asked the question, 'what if?' and then considered the fantastic possibilities. Through the imagination one can engage in problem solving and perhaps come to terms with reality. That is, the solutions to the problems of the outer world may be lying dormant in the inner world of the mind.

Figure 2.1

Figure 2.2

11

Understanding self and others

Through story, the interactions between people are revealed. How they love, show kindness or jealousy, offer friendship, compete and trick are revealed in many ways, simple and complex. Story provides examples of social contexts in which children can see real-life relationships between themselves and others being acted out and resolved in the literary world. This 'acting out' provides children with a range of options to consider when it comes to understanding their own motives and actions, as well as those of friends, parents and significant others in their lives. Britton (1979) says that if a story is close to a child's experience it will 'strengthen and confirm' that child's view of the world. Stories can be used to give children reference points for their experiences. This is true not only of literary stories but also of children's own stories, when these are given voice; they will provide opportunities for children to reflect on events and make sense of the experience. Tough (1974) believes that unless children are given opportunities to tell their stories, they may never come to understand or give meaning to them.

Much of the potential for gaining a better understanding of self and others will be lost if there is not time for reflection. Barbara Reed (1987, p. 36), who has worked with children in classroom storytelling, says that 'the youngsters needed time to process what they had heard'. In order to 'process' what the story tells them, children need to be provided with a number of different extension strategies. A wide range of these is described in the 'Practical activities' sections of this book. The children's individual preferences or learning styles need to be taken into account, however. Some children will need time to reflect on their own without any adult guidance or intervention; for others, strategies such as creative dramatics can be a means whereby children act out and role-play characters' thoughts and actions.

Story enables children to give shape to their life experiences through recounting them, or to compare them with similar experiences from literary sources. This is what Berger and Luckman (1966) call the 'imaginative construction' of everyday events.

Developing skills

It is difficult and indeed inappropriate to think of learning as occurring in either just the cognitive or the affective domain. Vygotsky's theory states that 'development does not proceed toward socialisation but toward the conversion of social relations into mental functions' (1962, p. 165). Children's social interaction with family, other adults and peers develops a

12

cognitive framework of perceptions about their personal, physical and social worlds. That framework will grow with each new experience and thus make possible the advancement of children's intellectual development (McNamee et al. 1985).

Exposure to stories, heard or viewed, enables children to extend their knowledge of story schema; that is, to establish expectations as to what will occur in the story (Nessel 1984). This ability to predict forms part of children's understanding or comprehension of story events. For example in the story of *The Gingerbread Man* (Ireson 1963) young children know that the fox intends eating the gingerbread man before the storyteller mentions it. They draw on prior experiences with stories where foxes are cunning tricksters and overconfident characters meet their match. There is also a rudimentary understanding of story climax which helps to prepare them for the outcome. Storytelling provides children with opportunities to develop listening comprehension skills, which are prerequisites for later reading comprehension. When storytelling is combined with judicious questioning and retelling strategies, comprehension skills at the literal, inferential and critical levels can be developed (Dwyer 1988). When children are engaged in the social function of storytelling they are learning to listen, to participate in and to understand story language or narrative discourse. These three skills are important in assisting children with the mechanics of reading and writing, which are not to be seen as ends in themselves, but as pathways to the more sophisticated use of language in everyday life.

Communication

Storytelling in its simplest form is learnt early by children; mastery can be a lifetime process. Young children employ storytelling in its many forms to entertain, explain or get attention and as part of everyday conversation (in gossiping, telling about outings with friends and so on). Garnett (1986) says that as children we learn to tell stories as a means of coming to know, to be known, and to share what we know. Christopher at 3 years of age would entertain his family every morning with long, often disconnected discourses about his dreams of the night before. The more his family responded to his stories with questions, shocked expressions and amused looks the more elaborate and extended his stories became. His family were acknowledging his tellings as 'fact'. This morning ritual became an important means by which he could guarantee a captive audience and reaffirm his place as a loved member of the family; it also helped develop his linguistic and oral skills.

Children come to preschool and school with their own stories to tell. These personal stories are based on their lives within their own social and cultural groups and, as such, may or may not reflect the social and cultural fabric of the dominant or mainstream group in society (Erasmus 1989). Sister Maria Jose Hobday (1979) tells the story of what happened one night when she was nearly 10 years old. It was late and she was walking home alone down the dimly lit street when out from behind some bushes jumped a man wielding a knife. She recognised him as Crazy Tom, a man given to wild escapades when drunk. He yelled and wildly ran after her with the knife. She ran home as fast as she could. Panting heavily, she ran to her father, who sat reading in the rocking chair. 'Daddy, Daddy!' she cried. 'Crazy Tom's chasing me with a knife.' Her father lowered the paper slowly and said quietly, 'Well, he didn't catch you, did he? I always said you were a good runner.' This response shocked her, but she soon realised that her father was right — and, moreover, that he had defused the entire experience. She says that suddenly she felt it was a great experience, worth telling everyone as soon as she could. Many people hearing this story might question the parents' responsibility in allowing their young daughter to go out on her own at night and walk home alone. The father's response could also be interpreted as uncaring. However, this was not how Maria perceived it. For her, the reply her father offered was a compliment that also helped her see the experience in another light. She says: 'what could have become a crippling experience was a victory, a show of courage. I knew Daddy approved of my fast sprint.'

As teachers we have a responsibility to respond positively to all children's stories because they offer important clues for understanding who the children are and what dreams and desires they have. Erasmus (1989, p. 273) says that 'when a person's discourse is devalued, so too are the meanings, experiences, and knowledge to which that discourse refers'. We run the risk of inhibiting children's development in the narrative form of communication unless we listen carefully to what they are telling us and accept and respond to their stories. Personal discourse is a necessary and important precursor to literary discourse. By sanctioning children's role as storytellers we enable them to communicate genuinely to others not only their stories, but much about themselves as people. Communication through storytelling results in the use of paralinguistic features (gestures, facial expressions) as well as linguistic features (use of tense, linking devices, clarification of ambiguity). The former tell the audience something about the person telling the story and the latter demonstrate how oral language, given a purposeful context, reveals a sophistication that goes beyond the level of conversation.

Empowering

When children tell stories they become aware of the power of their words. The language they use, be it their own or another's, will have an effect on the listeners. But there is also another kind of power, the kind that is manifested when a teller is in control of the experience and can choose how to respond to the needs of the audience. The faces of the audience and their utterances provide feedback to the teller, who responds accordingly by modifying vocal tone, facial expression, gesture, pace, body language and words. Schwartz (1987, p. 607) says that 'the most empowering part of storytelling lies not in the recollecting or learning but in the sharing'. A significant part of this sharing occurs when the teller connects with the listeners through the eyes.

Dwayne told his 12-year-old classmates the tale 'In a Dark, Dark Wood'. He adopted the pose, facial expression and voice of the archetypal Frankenstein monster. His voice was robotic in its monotone. His classmates were immediately drawn into his story, but instead of being 'frightened' they began to laugh. Dwayne responded to their laughter by becoming even more dramatic and 'over the top'. When he finished the story, his audience broke into spontaneous applause and said how much they liked the way he told it. Dwayne was satisfied that his storytelling was successful — and achieved a new status in the class.

An important byproduct of storytelling is a new level of confidence and self-esteem for the teller. Even the shyest child, when given the opportunity to share a story with another person, finds acceptance of both story and self a rewarding experience. Indeed, an important aim of nurturing children as storytellers is to help them develop confidence in themselves as communicators, and a sense of self-worth in their ability to share stories with their peers.

Literary conventions

Knowledge of literary conventions (e.g. point of view, plot, style, characterisation, setting, theme) is learnt and applied to other forms of written and oral narratives. As mentioned previously, storytelling helps children to read and write because it gives them frameworks or schema for understanding text. A 'sense of story' is a prerequisite not only for comprehension but also for producing different types of story. When children are exposed to different genres of literature they soon learn to expect certain features of that genre; for example the folktale with its conventional beginning of 'Once upon a time' and its problem-resolution story structure. Once children's awareness of narrative discourse is heightened they can apply this knowledge to their own reading, writing and storytelling. Phrases, expressions and language patterns are borrowed from stories heard and incorporated into their own stories. Three-year-old Thomas described a boy who had been mean to his sister at school as being just like 'John Stoat Ferret', a nasty character from Beatrix Potter's *The Tale of Mister Tod* (1986).

Too often children in schools are expected to write narratives before they have had a chance to develop the story both mentally and orally. When storytelling is part of the language curriculum, then children develop an understanding of story structure and organisation which can form a framework for their own stories. Syntactic structure can also be used as a reference framework for creating their own stories. According to King and McKenzie (1988, p. 307), children develop an 'intuitive awareness of authorship'. This intuition becomes more conscious as children begin to attend to the way the author uses words: the author's 'voice'. The same applies to storytelling. Children tune in to the storyteller's words and often incorporate these words and phrases into their own retellings. Conversely, children often successfully substitute their own words, phrases and expressions in a familiar story as they attempt to retain its original structure while giving it their own voice.

Environment

The classroom environment must be one where children feel that there is respect for them both as people and as storytellers. This means that they need to realise that their life experiences make them unique, and that these experiences are acknowledged and accepted by others. If children feel that somehow they don't quite measure up to others' expectations or standards of dress, speech and behaviour, then they will not feel comfortable about sharing their stories.

In preschool and the lower primary grades there does not appear to be the same problem of acceptance as is apparent in the later years of primary school and early secondary school. The power of the peer group is firmly established by about 10 years of age, when there may be intense pressure for children to confirm to certain codes of behaviour and dress. When it comes to acceptance or rejection, adolescent girls may be particularly vulnerable to the whims of their peers, of both sexes. The gender battle-lines are drawn in the upper primary grades and it becomes a difficult task for a teacher to develop mutual respect between boys and girls.

In one instance, a Year 7 class of 12 and 13 year-olds contained twenty-three boys and seven girls. Of the girls, only one had the confidence to volunteer to storytell in front of the whole class. The boys dominated and many were eager to 'go one better' than the previous male teller. There were also a few boys who tried to become 'invisible' and did not actively participate. One strategy which was used successfully to break down inhibition and fear of ridicule was to have the children work in pairs. This grouping was seen as less threatening and it gave those children who lacked confidence with a large audience the opportunity to achieve acceptance and encouragement on a one-to-one basis. Another strategy was to establish a process of positive feedback from the class when individuals told their stories. This helped to shift the focus from negative to positive criticism. It also promoted active listening on the part of the audience: there was an expectation that they would attend carefully not only to the story, but also to how it was told.

There are other more subtle ways in which the hidden 'gender' curriculum (Gilbert 1989) operates in schools. Teachers' expectations concerning the types of stories that boys and girls like to read and, consequently, to write and tell, often reinforce existing stereotypes. There is a common assumption among teachers and some academics that girls don't mind listening to stories about males but that boys won't have anything to do with 'sissy' or female stories (Spender 1978; Huck, Hepler & Hickman 1987). Even the sources of traditional literature (folktales and fairytales, myths and legends) need to provide children with alternatives to the 'weak damsel/strong prince' story characters which are so prolific. The 'Resources' chapter at the end of this book offers a good selection of unstereotypic stories about males and females.

'Environment' therefore includes both people and resources. Both need to be addressed resolutely.

In conclusion, the benefits that can be gained from encouraging children to be storytellers go way beyond the level of entertainment. There are positive social, emotional and intellectual rewards for children when we give them the time, space and opportunity to share their oral stories.

Practical activities

Getting started

Before you embark on storytelling with children it is important that you are confident in your own storytelling ability and familiar with a range of stories that you can encourage your students to explore.

The school library is the obvious starting point. Explore the folklore section and extend your knowledge and repertoire of these stories. Other sources for stories are audiotapes and videos of stories — preferably told, not read. Popular films on video, cartoons, jokes and songs are also important narrative sources.

Contact the Storytelling Guild in your State (see page 88). Members may be able to visit your class and tell stories.

Classroom environment

A special storyteller's chair can be brought into the classroom and decorated by the children. The chair is endowed with a special importance and is used by child and adult tellers. Other ritual props could include a special rug for children to sit on when stories are to be shared.

If children are comfortable sitting on the floor when storytelling, this is preferable and more informal; desks tend to act as barriers between teller and audience.

Visualisation activities

These encourage children to use their imaginations and allow the spoken word to create stories in their heads.

It is important that children be relaxed before beginning these activities. A darkened, quiet room is ideal. Ask them to lie on their backs on the floor and close their eyes. Give them a few minutes to settle in to the silence around them. Some simple breathing exercises can help them relax and shed any feelings of self-consciousness.

Tell a story, one you know or one have created yourself. Before you begin, tell the children you want them to see the story in their minds as you tell it. Afterwards ask the children to tell you what they visualised: for example what the characters looked like, their clothes, how they felt at different points in the story, the setting. This is best done in small groups or pairs as this allows all children to contribute.

Variation: Using familiar images. Ask children to relax, close their eyes and try to 'see' someone who is special to them who is not in the room. Ask them to visualise this person in a favourite chair or a particular room or place. Next ask them to visualise what that special person is wearing, doing or even saying.

Communication activities

These activities are designed to relax the children and to provide them with a variety of fun activities which focus on everyone's contribution to oral

18

sharing. They should be non-threatening and a foster a sense of community and cooperation.

Who stole the cookie from the cookie jar?

This familiar rhyme can be used to establish a relaxed atmosphere. Have everyone sit in a circle and clap hands twice then slap knees twice, to establish a group rhythm. When the rhythm is coordinated, begin the rhyme:

> ALL: Who stole the cookie from the cookie jar?
> LEADER: Megan stole the cookie from the cookie jar.
> MEGAN: Who, me? Couldn't be!
> ALL: Then who stole the cookie from the cookie jar?
> MEGAN: Bill stole the cookie from the cookie jar.

. . . and so on, until everyone has had a turn.

And then what happened?

This activity allows the group to develop a composite story and at the same time apply elements of story structure as the story develops from a beginning through a climax to a conclusion.

Children sit in a circle. You will need a soft ball: the person holding it tells a part of a story before passing on the ball. The first person begins a story, for example: 'Late one night, an old man was walking home'. The ball is then passed to the next person, who takes up the story; and so on until the last person in the circle receives the ball and has to bring the story to its conclusion.

The more often children do this activity the more skilful they will become at building up climax and anticlimax, humour, surprise twists and other narrative features.

That's a good story!

Divide the class into two groups, A and B. Give group A three or four key words from a story or joke that you know. Group A then leaves the room and is given no more than ten minutes to develop a group story around these words.

Group B remains in the room and is told the whole story or joke. When group A returns, each person has to tell the story to a person from group B, and vice versa.

It is interesting to finish this activity by listening to the different interpretations of both stories. This exercise is useful in showing children how stories change with each new telling.

That's good ... That's bad

Before this activity have all the children make simple puppets out of plastic flyswats, with a happy face on one side and a sad face on the other. Materials such as wool, paper, wood shavings, felt pens and adhesives can be used.

Model a story where a fortunate event is followed by an unfortunate event. As you tell the story, show the happy face of the puppet for the good thing and the sad face for the bad thing, and have the children do likewise.

Have the children sit in a circle with their puppets. Select a volunteer to begin a story (one or two sentences only). The story begins, for example:

FIRST CHILD: When I was going home from school yesterday I found a $10 note.
ALL: That's good!
SECOND CHILD: So I put the money in my pocket and walked to the shops. But there was a hole in my pocket and I lost the money.
ALL: That's bad!

... and so on, alternating good and bad fortune throughout the story while maintaining a logical sequence of events. The person speaking displays the happy or sad face of the puppet, as appropriate, and the others follow suit.

The puppets are not essential, but they provide children with a prop which may add a sense of fun to the activity and for some will give a feeling of security.

Variation. Individual children take turns to tell their own good fortune/bad fortune story.

Creative dramatics

Tell 'Oonagh and the Giant Cucullin' from *A Book of Giants* (Mayne 1972). This is a very funny story which tells how Oonagh, the wife of the giant Fin MacCoul, tricked the giant Cucullin into believing that Fin was stronger than he.

After the story have children pretend they are giants and imagine how they might behave (e.g. eating a whole roast), how they would walk, talk and so on. Allow plenty of space for the children to move around during this role-playing.

Next, have the children form groups of four. Within each group the children can assign the following characters: Fin, Oonagh, Cucullin and a reporter from a television news program. Each group plans a role-play where the reporter interviews each of the other three characters about the events of the story. Later they may share their role-plays with the class.

This activity is helpful not only for developing recall of story events but also for interpreting the feelings and motives of characters in the story.

Chapter 3

FINDING THE STORIES TO TELL

Eric the dinosaur had a little chip on his tooth.
He must have been a muttaburrasaurus. He
liked to eat plants, leaves, branches, trees. Then
he ate meat. Because he was really a meat-eater.
Then he died.

Christopher, aged 4

Finding the right story to tell need not be difficult. Children are natural storytellers and often tell each other stories, jokes and riddles. Tapping into this reservoir of everyday storytelling is the best starting point. In pairs or small groups, children can share a story about something that happened to them over the weekend; a story about when they were little; something that happened to a family member or a friend.

Before they reach the stage where they are ready to retell stories from books, children need to read or listen to many different stories. We can recommend books to help children in their search, but ultimately it is up to the storyteller to make that very individual selection. Ruth Sawyer (1976), a distinguished storyteller, says that the relationship between a story and teller is 'as personal as the clothes we wear'.

Finding the right story takes time: time to read, time to reflect, time to share and time to discard if necessary and begin again. Children need to be given this time to explore stories and they also need a wide range of quality narratives from which they can begin their discoveries. They can only learn to be discriminating in their selections through exposure to many different types of literature.

For all storytellers, the challenge is to find a story which you not only like, but also understand and want to share with others. Often our understanding of a story deepens with each reading or telling. This growing familiarity with story is part of the storytelling process. Sometimes you come across a story which you like and want to tell. However, the telling may never live up to your expectations: the audience did not respond as you thought they would; or your voice never seemed to achieve the desired effects. It may mean you need to work at making this story more personal, or let it go for a while and come back to it some other time.

Elements of a good story

When looking for a good story to tell, keep the following points in mind:

1 Quick beginning. A quick beginning will grab the audience's attention. Avoid lengthy, obscure beginnings. Children enjoy hearing stories which get on with the action, not those which just meander along. The beginning is often the most difficult part of the storytelling and the teller needs to make sure that the beginning is clear and confidently told.

2 Straightforward action. The action needs to be direct, flowing easily and simply from one event to the next. Avoid stories with too many subplots and digressions.

3 Definite climax. The plot should have a definite climax. This is something that listeners expect of a story. The plot needs to be leading somewhere and the build-up to the climax can be heightened by the storyteller's skill and the innate power of the story.

4 Limited number of characters. Look for stories where the number of characters is limited to about three or four. The novice storyteller should not try to use a different voice for each character as this might be too difficult to sustain. Instead, try modulating the voice for different effects. Many folktales have a limited number of characters and are ideal for beginners.

5 Repetitive pattern. Stories which have a repetitive pattern — 'Run, run, as fast as you can, you can't catch me I'm the gingerbread man' — are easy to tell. Repetitive patterns provide a linchpin for the events in the story, as well as an opportunity for audience participation. The recurring phrases or events also act as aids for understanding and memory, for both teller and listener.

6 Satisfying conclusion. A satisfying conclusion is most appreciated by young children, who like to see justice prevailing and wrongdoers receiving their just desserts; they do not favour stories that leave the problem unresolved. With some stories, the audience may need time to assimilate the ending. It is important for the storyteller to allow a few minutes for this to happen and not be disappointed if there was not the expected reaction at the end of the telling.

For example 'The Yellow Ribbon' (Ferguson & Durkin 1989), a story with a surprise ending, was told to a Year 7 class. In this story, Sam and Susannah have known each other since they were babies and have been married for many, many years. Susannah has always worn a yellow ribbon around her neck but has never told Sam why. Then on her deathbed she gives him permission to undo the ribbon: 'So Sam untied the ribbon and ... her head fell OFF!' There was absolute silence for several seconds afterwards, before the children started to respond verbally. On another occasion when this story was told to an adult audience, there was a spontaneous burst of laughter after the final words were spoken.

7 Different versions. Look for different tellings of the same story in order to find the version with which you feel most comfortable. Some traditional stories do not read well, but come alive when spoken. The storyteller's ability to embellish and interpret the story gives colour and life to such stories. After all, these stories were meant to be told. Many picture-book stories are difficult to tell because appreciation of them depends on the combination of text and illustrations. It is best to select a story which sounds like a story to be told, and does not need pictures to help interpret it.

Given these criteria, where do we begin looking for stories to tell?

Using everyday experiences

Children's everyday experiences are the best place to begin storytelling.

Children's folklore

Non-narrative sources of children's folklore (riddles, jokes, tongue twisters etc.) can be useful starting points for young storytellers. There is little need to select books for the children on this topic as the school playground is a lively source buzzing with plenty of examples. For generations children have had their own inventive and imaginative parodies, riddles and jokes. Remember this one?

> *Adam and Eve and Pinch-me*
> *Went down to the river to bathe.*
> *Adam and Eve were drowned —*
> *Who do you think was saved?*

25

Research into children's folklore has revealed a fascinating range of material. The 'Resources' chapter cites several books on this topic; no doubt every classroom could extend the contents of these books.

Personal experience stories

Children's personal stories build on from their oral folklore. Anecdotes and extended retellings of everyday events about family, friends, toys and pets provide the basis for these stories. Personal experience stories are often best told in small groups or to a partner because their very nature means that the storyteller is sharing something personal, which may make some children uncomfortable in a large group. A straight retelling of an experience can be dull and lifeless because the teller is aware of the factual nature of the account. Some children may need to be encouraged to exaggerate and embellish their stories in order to entertain their audience. The 'tall tale' is a type of firsthand folktale that contains a large dose of poetic licence and colourful language. Children can employ this style of storytelling when relating a personal experience.

Personal creative stories

These stories are the direct product of the storyteller's imagination. A real person or event may provide the basis for the story, or it may revolve around a fictitious character or a favourite stuffed toy, doll or family pet.

Traditional sources

Folktales

This is a generic term which includes legends, ballads, epics, sagas, myths and fables. Fairytales are often put in this category, but these are more modern, fanciful stories created by a known writer, such as Hans Christian Andersen.

For our purposes, folktales will refer to those stories originating from the oral tradition, i.e. stories told by the common folk.

Folktales are the easiest stories to tell. They come from two sources: the oral story tradition and the written story, handed down through the years. Many cultures, for example Aboriginal people, have an oral record of stories. These are passed on from generation to generation, by word of mouth. Many of these stories have now been written down, making them accessible to a wide audience. The small picture books of Aboriginal Dreaming tales compiled by Pamela Lofts and those written by Dick Roughsey and Percy Tresize are very popular with primary age children.

Other written stories have been collected from many different cultures. Collectors of folktales and fairytales include the Brothers Grimm (stories from Germany), Joseph Jacobs (from England), Charles Perrault (from France), Virginia Tashjian (from Armenia), Virginia Haviland (from many countries), Diane Wolkstein (from Haiti), Grace Hallworth (from the West Indies), Bill Scott (from Australia). These stories are the written products of countless retellings and reshapings.

Folktales are generally enjoyed because of their familiar structure. Their universal structure of setting-problem-events-resolution-conclusion makes them easily understood and tellable.

The language of folktales is usually strong, simple and vigorous. After all, the words are very important for impact in these relatively short stories. Consider the opening lines in the story 'Owl' in *The Magic Orange Tree* (Wolkstein 1978, p. 31):

Owl thought he was very ugly. But one evening he met a girl and talked with her and she liked him. 'If it had been day', Owl thought, 'and she had seen my face, she never would have liked me'. But still she had liked him.

From the very beginning, the audience is introduced to the protagonist and knows how he feels about himself. Owl's insecurity is the underlying theme to this sad tale of love lost.

The subject matter of folktales is universally recognisable. The themes of many tales reflect our personal desires, insecurities, ambitions, fears. They speak directly to our emotions and intellect. The subject matter is also a source for valid criticism of this genre. Writers such as Jack Zipes (1986) and Pam Gilbert (1989) have criticised the implicit messages about gender roles and personalities of males and females. For example stepmothers are often mean and cruel, witches are evil and ugly, princesses are often beautiful victims waiting to be saved by a handsome prince, and most of the stories are about the adventures of men and boys. Most folktales, especially those stemming from the European tradition, have been collected and written by men, though women were often the storytellers. Given the social contexts of the times when they were recorded (mainly the last century), these collections generally reflect a dominant male ideology. The 'Resources' chapter cites several collections which feature female characters who are good and brave counterparts to the male characters common to many folktales.

The stereotyping of characters by gender is one feature of folktales, but there is also the stereotyping of character traits. The good are usually good and the bad are awful. This dichotomous distinction of moral inclination reflects the level of moral reasoning of many 6–8 year-olds, and this age group is the most appreciative of folktales. Older children's interests broaden to include myths, epics and sagas.

Myths

Myths are narratives which give explanations about the origins of natural and social phenomena, or accounts of interactions between humans and supernatural beings. Myths are quite demanding to tell, yet there is a powerful attraction in these gutsy, action-packed tales. The appeal of recent films like *Mad Max, Raiders of the Lost Ark* and others of that genre bears testimony to the popularity of hero-quest tales.

Like folktales, these stories are largely populated by male heroes of semi-divine nature. There are, however, many tales about heroic women. Maurice Saxby's complementary volumes *The Great Deeds of Super Heroes* (1989) and *Tales of Heroic Women* (1990) offer good retellings of myths and redress the balance of male and female heroes. These stories are not for the beginning storyteller, however, as they are demanding to tell because of their intricate plot structure, language and tempo. Ruth Sawyer (1976) has referred most appositely to the function and appeal of these stories as being able to 'charm the ear and arrest the mind'.

Fables

Fables are short, didactic stories, usually with a moral or lesson which is the point of the tale. Because of their short length, few characters and single-incident format, they are ideal for beginner storytellers. The fable's appeal lies in its abstraction of a generalisation from a specific incident — 'slow and steady wins the race'. Because of this fables appeal most to children in the middle to upper primary grades and upwards.

The most common fables are those of Aesop and La Fontaine. However, children should be able to hear and read fables from other countries, like India. There are many retellings which employ embellished storylines and modern conversational style. *Foxy Fables* (Ross 1986) has a modern-day flavour:

> *Madame Crow was very large and glossy black. When she was a small crowlet, someone told her that she had a lovely voice (for a crow), and ever since then she had fancied herself as an opera singer. She was an unbearable crow.*

Contemporary retellings make fables more accessible for many children, but this is not to say that children should not hear the more traditional

28

versions. Both have their place. Some contemporary writers convey their themes or messages in what could be termed 'modern fables'. Leo Lionni draws on a Hindu tale in his story *Tico and the Golden Wings* (1975); and his *Frederick* (1971) can be considered a modern fable because of its moral message.

The Bible

The Bible is a fine source of parables, proverbs and interesting characters. The Bible as literature is considered essential for all children by literary scholars such as Northrop Frye. According to Frye (1964), through the Bible we learn about our humanity and the universal, timeless search for truth and meaning. Using the Bible as a source of literature is quite different from using it as a vehicle for religious indoctrination. There are some handsome picture-book stories from the Old Testament; see the 'Resources' chapter for some of these.

All religions have their stories. Teachers can include a variety of these to make Australian children aware of their multicultural heritage.

The 'Resources' chapter suggests books which reflect the range discussed in this chapter. Consider it a starting point only. Share it with your children and encourage them to add to it.

People as sources

Finally, remember that people — neighbours, family, teachers, librarians and, of course, children — are sources for stories, and just as important as written sources. All storytellers need to keep their ears and eyes ever alert for a new story to tell.

Practical activities

Memories

- Children may interview grandparents, parents, friends and neighbours and record the memories they relate: family anecdotes; stories about school life, games, toys. Children may share these stories in a small group or with a partner.

- Read *Wilfrid Gordon MacDonald Partridge* (Fox 1985). Ask children to talk about some things they remember — something happy, something scary . . .

- Talk about the association between colour and memory; for example, warm colours reflect happy memories. Make up a colour wheel of memory stories. Children could draw a picture to represent their own memory story.

Personal histories

Encourage children to keep a scrapbook of things that happen to them throughout the year. Entries could include drawings, photographs or writings about dreams, parties, school events, favourite stories. They may share these stories from time to time with selected members of the class.

Jokes and riddles

Collect jokes, riddles and the popular verses found in autograph books, for example:

> Roses are red,
> Cabbages are green
> My face may be funny
> But yours is a scream!

Share these and keep favourite examples in a class book with accompanying illustrations.

Neighbourhood legends

Children love to tell stories about people and places in their neighbourhood. Often these stories are part of local folklore. Draw a large map of the local area and pinpoint places which have a story to be told. This activity also encourages a sense of community.

Magical items

Look for stories where characters have a lucky charm or magical item, for example:

'One Eye, Two Eyes, Three Eyes' (Arbuthnot 1961) — magic goat
'The Lad Who Went to the North Wind' (Asbjornsen & Moe 1963) — magic tablecloth
Strega Nona (de Paola 1975) — magic pasta pot
Snow White and the Seven Dwarfs (Grimm & Grimm 1975a) — magic mirror

Children can share these stories with each other and investigate the lucky charms that people have today.

Superstitions

Many stories concern superstitions and the curse that befalls people who break the rules associated with local beliefs. Share some of these stories, for example:

The White Crane (Morimoto 1983) — transformation of crane to girl and back again
'Urashimo Taro' (Sakade 1964) — opens box and is returned to former world
'Pandora's Box' (White 1964) — opens box and releases all the objects of desire

Children can ask their parents, grandparents and friends about their superstitions (never walk under a ladder; don't open an umbrella in the house) and discover the stories behind them.

Point of view

Find a folktale or fable and retell it from a different point of view. For example retell *The Hare and the Tortoise* (La Fontaine 1966) from the hare's point of view. Children can prepare a paired storytelling, with each person telling the story from their character's point of view. *There's a Wolf in My Pudding* (Wilson 1986) is a good book for this strategy. Children are quick to pick up the idea and can invent some funny interpretations.

Variation. Alter the characters' personalities and see how the story changes. For example how different would *Cinderella* be if the stepsisters were shy and Cinderella was a spoilt brat?

Character cards

Keep a box or file of characters from different stories with a brief description of each character. One side of the card gives the character description, for example: 'Owl — shy, lacks confidence, thinks himself ugly.' The other side gives the title and author: 'Owl', in *The Magic Orange Tree* by Diane Wolkstein.

Children can tell a group story by selecting three or four different characters cards and building a story around them. This activity involves children in problem solving, working cooperatively and employing knowledge of story structure.

Beginnings

On cards, write folktale beginnings, for example:

Once upon a time . . .
Once there was and once there wasn't . . .
Long, long ago in . . . there lived a . . .
There was once a very rich . . .

These cards can be displayed across a wall for children to use when creating their own stories to tell.

Children's museum

Set up a children's museum in the classroom or school library. Include toys, games and craft items popular in years gone by. If actual items are difficult to find, children could make some of them. An excellent book on the history of folk art is *Toys and Tales from Grandmother's Attic* (Kraska 1979).

Story corner

Set up a table in the classroom for children to contribute objects of interest — a shell, an old doll, a photograph, a hat, an old-fashioned key . . . These items can act as stimuli for storytelling ideas. Once the stories have been told they can be written down for others to read.

Newspaper stories

Local newspapers can be a rich source of story ideas. Keep a file of newspaper clippings of stories about local heroes, unsolved mysteries, lost pets, funny incidents. Children could be encouraged to talk about these and develop their own oral stories from them. Writers often use this strategy for their stories; for example Allan Baillie's *Adrift* (1984) was inspired by an incident reported in a newspaper.

Interviews with folktale characters

Children are naturally curious and often ask questions about what they hear or read. Use this curiosity to develop their imaginations with 'what if?' questions:

- What would happen if Perseus, Rapunzel and Cinderella met at a restaurant (disco/park/your home)? What would they talk about? What questions would you like to ask them?

Children can explore these ideas in small groups. They need to be familiar with the stories about these characters first.

32

Chapter 4

LEARNING THE STORIES

Once there was, and once there was not . . .

'How do you remember all the story?' This is probably the most common question asked of storytellers. The fear of not being able to remember the details of a story is a common one for most people and becomes an inhibiting factor in their own ventures into storytelling. Storytelling, like music, dance and theatre, is a performing art, and the performers need to be taught how to approach their art to achieve the best results.

Developing a story memory

Teachers can teach children strategies for developing story memory. Story memory does not mean learning a story word for word, sentence for sentence. It does mean developing an understanding of story structure.

Top-level structure

We teach children about top-level structure to help them understand written text and organise information into a meaningful plan or framework. Unless we have a plan or framework for learning, our efforts will be wasted. Part of our organising plan or framework for remembering a story is to understand its top-level structure. We do this by breaking the story into smaller chunks and giving each chunk a name or special significance. These chunks are then broken down further, and further again, until the story has a framework with which our memory can cope.

Chunking

Chunking helps us to group and categorise story events. We apply this chunking process every day without consciously realising it, for example by breaking down telephone numbers into smaller sequences for easier recall. Children are taught the alphabet through a rhyming song which divides the twenty-six letters into sets of chunks (*abcdefg, hijklmnop* . . .), which are further subdivided (*ab, cd, ef, g, hi, jk, lmno, p* — and so on).

Visualisation

Another method of memory training is the process of visualisation. Recall is achieved by visualising or reconstructing the story in 'scenes in the mind'. These scenes may even be given a physical location. For example children can take each scene from a story and assign it to a different part of the room, so that when they look at or imagine a part of the room they will recall the relevant scene. This technique is an extension of the ancient Greek method of memory training where items are memorised by placing them in different locations. The poet Simonides is credited with inventing the technique, called the *method of loci* (Norman 1969).

Here are some ways of applying these ideas to help children remember story content.

Story structure

Many stories have a structure. The structure is an organisational framework which makes 'story' what it is. People recognise story because they have come to expect certain features of this type of discourse: language, sequence of events, recurring themes, ritual beginnings ('Once upon a time') and endings ('And they never came back again').

Even very young children, with their limited experiences of literature, know intuitively that stories have a beginning, a middle and an end. Figure 4.1 shows a basic story frame or structure.

Beginning	Setting and characters Introduce problem
Middle	Event sequence: 1. 2. 3. Resolution of problem
End	Conclusion Moral

Figure 4.1. Basic story frame

The basic story frame can be expanded to show children that within the three broad divisions we are given other information about the story (see figure 4.2). The teacher can explain this by asking for a volunteer to retell a

34

familiar folktale such as 'The Three Billy Goats Gruff' (Asbjornsen & Moe 1963). After the storytelling children are asked what information they were told at the beginning of the story, in the middle, and at the end. Their responses are recorded. With careful guidance and appropriate questioning, children can come to see that the basic story frame can be expanded into smaller chunks to include more details about the story, as in figure 4.2.

This story frame can be transferred to a wallchart to act as a useful reference guide for the children when they are learning stories to retell and also when composing their own written narratives.

Beginning	**Setting and characters** 'Once upon a time there were three Billy Goats who were to go up to the hillside to make themselves fat, and the family name of the three goats was "Gruff".' **Problem** The billy goats had to cross a bridge under which lived a great ugly Troll.
Middle	**Sequence of events** 1 The youngest Billy Goat Gruff goes to cross the bridge —Trip, trap! Trip, trap! 2 The Troll lets him pass after he hears that second Billy Goat is bigger. 3 The second Billy Goat Gruff goes to cross the bridge — Trip, Trap! Trip, Trap! Trip, Trap! 4 Troll lets him pass when he hears that the third Billy Goat is bigger. 5 The biggest Billy Goat Gruff goes to cross the bridge — TRIP, TRAP! TRIP, TRAP! TRIP, TRAP! 6 He and the Troll fight. **Resolution of problem** The Troll is tossed in the river and drowns.
End	**Conclusion** ' . . . and the Billy Goats Gruff went up to the hillside and got so fat that they were scarcely able to walk home again! Snip, Snap, Snout, this tale's told out.'

Figure 4.2. Expanded story frame

Mapping story structure

The framework of a story can be represented, or mapped, in a number of different ways, depending on the underlying purpose and the type of story. According to Davis and McPherson (1989, p. 232), story mapping provides 'a graphic representation of all or part of the elements of a story and the relationships between them'. In the context of storytelling, the main function of story mapping is to serve as a memory aid, by providing children with a visual and practical aid for organising story content.

The following examples include children's attempts to develop and use different story map formats.

Story webs

Children can use a story web to illustrate 'textually explicit' information from the story. There are basically two approaches to story webs. One is to draw a number of circles on a page in which to write key words or brief phrases from a story. These are connected with lines to show the story sequence. In figure 4.3, Tamie's story web of 'Old One Eye' (MacDonald 1986) highlights the circular nature of the tale.

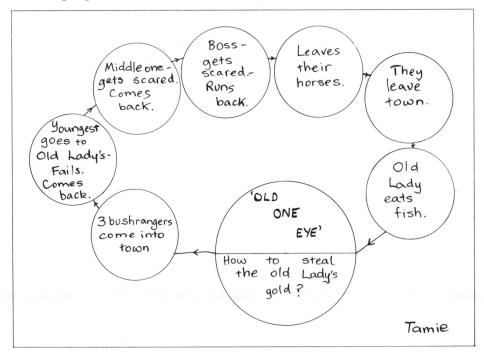

Figure 4.3. Tamie's story web

36

The second approach is more structured. Children use a problem-setting bubble as the starting point; the main events are then organised chronologically in bubbles, starting from the left of the problem bubble and moving clockwise. In figure 4.4, Kurt attempts to do this with a story web of 'The Wide-Mouth Frog' (Livo & Rietz 1986).

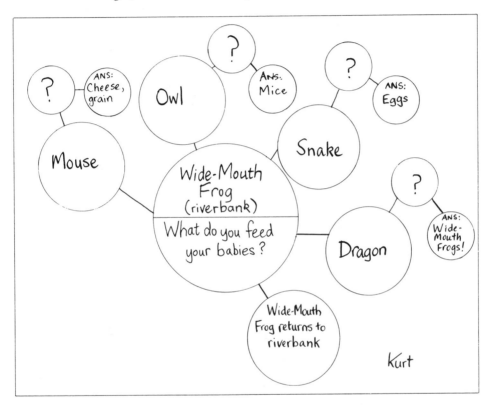

Figure 4.4. Kurt's story web

Many teachers and children will be familiar with story (or semantic) webs in other aspects of their language work. The application described here is for the purpose of remembering story sequence.

Storyboards

A storyboard is a series of 'frames' showing the events of the action. It may incorporate significant dialogue or repeated phrases, but usually features simple line drawings only. Charlene's storyboard of 'In a Dark, Dark Wood' (Ferguson & Durkin 1989) is shown in figure 4.5.

Figure 4.5. Charlene's storyboard

38

Story maps

A story map can be used to show the setting and the journey taken by characters in the story. This type of story map is particularly helpful for quest tales. The map can show the path of the action, and any significant dialogue or repeated phrases can be included, as in figure 4.6, Kurt's story map for 'The Gunny Wolf' (MacDonald 1986). Kurt has also used arrows to show the direction of the little girl's journey to and from the forest.

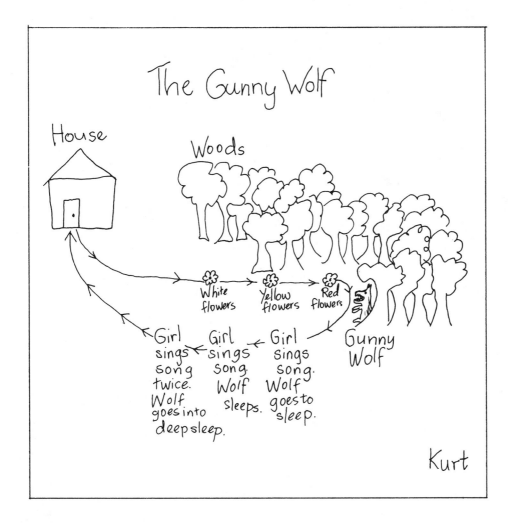

Figure 4.6. Kurt's story map

Dwayne's story map (figure 4.7) shows the journey in two styles, with a dotted line representing the journey into the forest and a solid line showing the journey home.

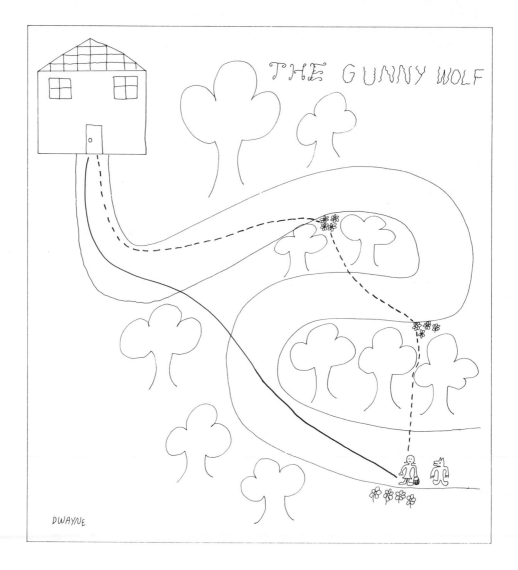

Figure 4.7. Dwayne's story map

Story cards

Some storytellers who are less visually oriented use notes on a story card to help them remember a story. The story card can be used to outline and number the major sequence of events in the story. Having children record on a card ensures that they do not write too much. The example in figure 4.8 is based on the simplified story frame model discussed earlier. Kimberley (aged 8) has given just the story sequence for 'The Yellow Ribbon' (Ferguson & Durkin 1989).

The Yellow Ribbon

1 They were babies and Sam asked Sue why she wore the yellow ribbon but Sue didn't tell him.

2 They were in Kindy and Sam asked Sue why she wore the yellow ribbon but she said, 'Mind your own business'.

3 They were in Year 1 and Sam asked Sue why she wore the yellow ribbon, while playing Mr Wolf. She said, 'Get lost'.

4 Go through Years 2, 3, 4, 5, 6.

5 Asks Sue again in Year 7. She says, 'Go away'.

6 Don't see each other for a long time.

7 Sam sees Sue in town and wants to marry her, she says yes.

8 Have lots of children and grandchildren and great-grandchildren and great-great-grandchildren.

9 Sue is about to die and lets Sam take off the yellow ribbon and . . .

10 HER HEAD FALLS OFF!

Figure 4.8. Kimberley's story card

Main ideas and supporting ideas

Alternatively, older children can be encouraged to list the main ideas and their supporting ideas as Alisha (aged 11) has done in figure 4.9 for the story of 'The Golden Leg' (Ferguson & Durkin 1989).

The Golden Leg

1 Rich lord marries a beautiful girl.
   (a) He gives her jewels, clothes, money.
   (b) They go to balls and parties.
2 Lady is skipping down the stairs getting ready to go to a ball and breaks her leg.
   (a) Doctor came and told the lord that it was broken in seven places.
   (b) Second doctor comes and says leg must be cut off.
3 Lord has a leg of gold made for his beautiful wife.
   (a) They are both happy.
   (b) Lord buys more clothes and jewels.
4 Seven years later she breaks her neck and dies.
   (a) They have a funeral.
   (b) Lord makes everyone in the household wear black clothes.
   (c) Valet decides to steal leg to make money.
5 Gravedigger hears a ghost calling for her leg of gold.
   (a) Lord goes to her grave.
   (b) Lady-in-waiting goes to grave.
   (c) Valet goes to grave.
6 Pulls valet into grave and eats him.

Figure 4.9. Main ideas and supporting ideas, by Alisha

Recognising story patterns

After the children's own personal stories, folktales are the best starting point for storytellers, both adults and children. Folktales have distinctive story patterns which help both the teller and the audience to remember and enjoy the story. The cumulative pattern is common to many folktales.

Cumulative stories

The main feature of cumulative stories is that elements (things, people or experiences) are added as the story progresses. For example in *The Fisherman and His Wife* (Grimm & Grimm 1970) the pattern is repeated six times as the wife makes the fisherman ask the magic fish to grant an ever greedier wish. Finally the fish refuses and the fisherman and his wife are back where they started, living in a hovel. This is also a circular story and children could map the story to show this pattern, as shown in figure 4.10.

The Fat Cat (Kent 1984) is an example of another type of cumulative tale where, as each new item is added, the list is repeated in chronological order:

> *I ate the gruel*
> *and the pot*
> *and the old woman, too,*
> *and Skohottentot*
> *and Skolinkenlot.*
> *And now I am going to also eat YOU.*

Because of their particular story patterns, cumulative stories offer children the opportunity to engage in language play by chanting or singing the repeated story events. These stories are very predictable and involve the audience in a game to guess where the plot is going and just how many times the pattern will be repeated. They also extend children's ability to memorise lists.

Other cumulative folktales include:

The Bremen Town Musicians (Grimm & Grimm 1968)
Why Mosquitoes Buzz in People's Ears (Aardema 1975)
This is the House That Jack Built (Underhill 1987)
Stone Soup (Brown 1947)
Epaminondas (Merriam 1968)
The Gingerbread Man (Ireson 1963)
The Great Big Enormous Turnip (Tolstoy 1968)

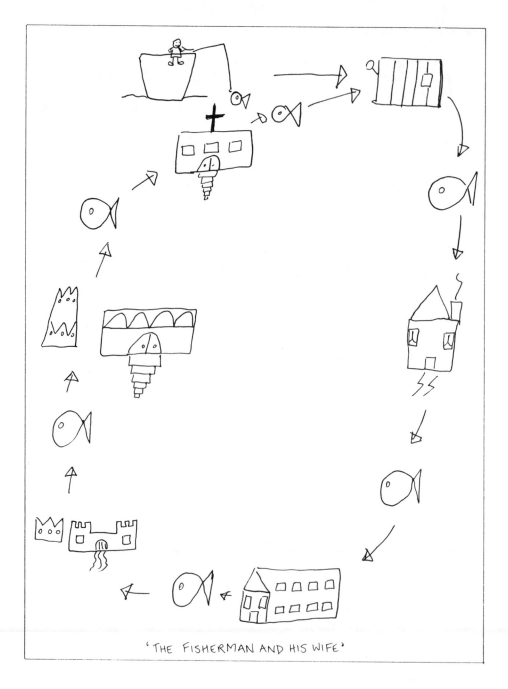

Figure 4.10. Story mapping: *The Fisherman and His Wife*

Sequential stories

Sequential stories are also highly predictable. This type of story organisation involves one event being repeated again and again. In *The Three Little
Pigs* (Peppé 1979), for example, each pig is confronted by the wolf, who
wants to eat it. The story sequence involves the wolf huffing, puffing,
blowing the house down, and eating the pig. This happens twice before the
third pig outwits the wolf. He does so three times, again repeating a
sequence of events: the pig arranges to meet the wolf at a certain time and
place; the pig arrives earlier than arranged; the pig gets food for himself;
the wolf becomes infuriated. This story also follows a number pattern of
three: three pigs; three visits to other places; the way the wolf tries to
destroy the pigs' homes (huffing, puffing and blowing).
   Folktales with a sequential pattern include:

'The Gunny Wolf' (MacDonald 1986)
'Molly Whuppie' (Ferguson & Durkin 1989)
'Coyote and the Crying Son' (MacDonald 1986)
'The Lad Who Went to the North Wind' (Asbjornsen & Moe 1963)
'The Tongue-Cut Sparrow' (Haviland 1969)
'The Three Billy Goats Gruff' (Asbjornsen & Moe 1963)

Chronicle pattern stories

The chronicle pattern story does not feature repetition of events, but the
story follows a logical sequence of cause and effect leading to the resolution. Some of the longer fairytales are good examples of the chronicle
pattern. Examples include:

Rapunzel (Grimm & Grimm 1960)
The Ugly Duckling (Andersen 1972)
The Monkey and the Crocodile (Galdone 1969)
'The Wonderful Pearl' (Riordan 1984)
The White Crane (Morimoto 1983)
'The White Bull of the Washpin' (Wannan 1974)
The Magic Tree (McDermott 1974)
'The Two Sisters' (Nielson & Nielson 1969)

Number pattern stories

Many traditional stories are organised not only in a conventional pattern
(e.g. cumulative or sequential) but also in a number pattern. For many
cultures this number has religious significance.

45

In European cultures the number 3 (and its multiples) is the most common; for example *The Three Little Pigs* (Peppé 1979), 'The Three Wishes' and 'Goldilocks and the Three Bears' (Garrity 1987), 'The Three Billy Goats Gruff' (Asbjornsen & Moe 1963). Other number patterns do occur, but far less frequently, for example 7: *The Fisherman and His Wife* (Grimm & Grimm 1970), *Hans in Luck* (Grimm & Grimm 1975*b*); and 9: *The Fat Cat* (Kent 1984). Encourage the children to find stories from other cultures, for example African and native American, to discover other number patterns.

Livo and Rietz (1986, p. 83) suggest that the number pattern of a story 'is an integral part of its top-level or discourse structure'. For instance *The Fat Cat* is a cumulative story based on the number 9 and therefore contains nine items in its cumulative list:

> *I ate the gruel*
> *and the pot*
> *and the old woman, too,*
> *and Skohottentot*
> *and Skolinkenlot*
> *and five birds in a flock*
> *and seven girls dancing*
> *and the lady with the pink parasol*
> *and the parson with the crooked staff.*

'Goldilocks and the Three Bears' (Garrity 1987) is a sequential story based on the number 3. The story contains three beds, three bowls, three chairs, three beds, three repetitive sets of language chanting and three problems (especially for Baby Bear).

The number patterns in stories are an aid to the teller's memory and help to organise the events in the overall story structure. This makes number pattern stories particularly suitable for beginning storytellers.

In conclusion, children can be shown a variety of strategies for learning stories. These strategies should be seen as flexible, not rigid; their appropriateness will depend on the child and the story.

In learning to retell stories, children will come to understand story structure and story language. This knowledge will also be useful when they come to write their own stories.

Practical activities

Sentence strips

Rewrite a nursery rhyme in single sentences, each on a strip of paper. Rearrange the strips and ask children to put them in order to make a story. This activity helps to reinforce the basic story structure of beginning, middle and end.

A natural extension of this activity is to use the children's stories, your own, or short folktales. For these longer stories break the story into reasonable chunks of text rather than sentences. You may model this activity first as a whole class activity for children to do later in pairs.

Number pattern stories

Ask children to compose orally a story based on a number (for example 3). Children could do this activity in groups of three to reinforce the number concept. First ask the children to consider the features of their story: three characters or items (such as a bird, a gold coin, a magic cape). Encourage the children to develop their story using the story frame as an organising tool.

Once they are successful at working stories in this way, increase the complexity of the story by having them develop their story with other sets of 3, for example three problems, three settings, three story episodes and so on.

Innovating on cumulative story structure

Children retell a cumulative story, substituting different characters or different items without losing the integrity of the original story.

Picture cards

On small cards, children draw pictures of the main events of their stories. These cards can be useful memory helpers when learning a story. When arranged side by side, they form a storyboard.

'Tree' stories

Share different number stories. Discuss the similarity of the basic story frame for each of the stories. Children can learn to retell number stories by drawing a tree with branches and clusters off the branches which represent that number.

For example a tree diagram for *The Three Little Pigs* would have three branches, with three clusters on each branch, reflecting the number pattern of the story (see figure 4.11).

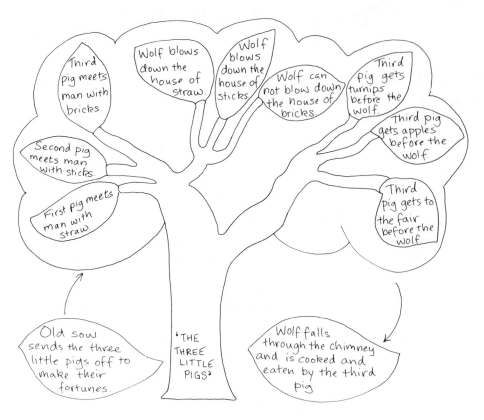

Figure 4.11. Tree story: *The Three Little Pigs*

Story artefacts and motifs

Give children different artefacts (a shell, an old key, a piece of embroidery) and ask them to make up stories which involve one or more of these objects. They will need plenty of time to exchange ideas and possibilities. Try to keep the activity oral rather than written.

Some storytellers use symbols and motifs in their storytelling outfits — a dress or cape embroidered with designs, a headband, a handbag decorated with patterns from a particular cultural group. The artefacts are also helpful props for remembering stories.

Children can design their own motifs or simply write a name (e.g. 'Anansi') on a small square of paper to represent a story they can tell. This can be glued on a class storytelling chart to show the range of stories that children and adults (teacher, parents, principal) can tell. It serves to remind individuals of their own repertoire.

48

Ball of wool

This is a shared storytelling experience. Children sit in a circle. The leader, holding a ball of wool, tells the first part of a story. She stops at an appropriate point in the story, holds one end of the wool and throws the ball to another person in the circle. That child tells the next part of the story and keeps hold of his section of the wool before throwing the ball to the next person. They continue in this way until the story is completed and children are all holding one part of the wool, symbolising the idea that each part of the story belongs to a teller.

Variations on story mapping

There are many ways of using story mapping, for different types of stories and different purposes.

Inferential story webs are an extension of the textually explicit type discussed in this chapter. Encourage children to explore the implied or unstated thoughts, feelings and reactions of a character or characters in a

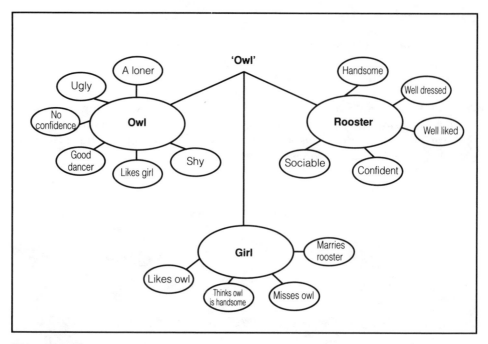

Figure 4.12

story. The story web in figure 4.12 was the result of a brainstorming session with children about the three characters in 'Owl' (Wolkstein 1978). This inference-making activity helps children to develop an understanding of characters which will in turn help them interpret characters when retelling a story.

Comparison-contrast story maps can be used in two ways:

- Use a semantic web format to show the advantages and disadvantages of being a certain character from a story.

- Compare and contrast feelings, strengths and weaknesses of different characters in a story.

Storyboard ideas

Prepare a storyboard of a story which the children already know. Cut the storyboard into its individual parts and ask children to rearrange the parts into the correct sequence. They can retell the story in pairs when this is done.

Variation. Give children a sheet of paper ruled up into squares in which you have drawn some parts of a story. Children complete the storyboard in pairs. You may use a familiar story, or have the children create a story from the few drawings they are given.

Murals

Children plot the sequence of a story on a sheet of paper. This can be presented as a mural showing the setting (and changes in setting). The mural can be used as a backdrop for retelling the story with puppets.

Songs

Share songs that have a cumulative structure (e.g. 'The Boy with the Drum', 'There's a Hole in the Bottom of the Sea') or a sequential structure ('The Bear Hunt'). Children can then create their own cumulative or sequential stories to sing or tell.

Peer tutoring

Peer tutoring is helpful in the early preparation stages of learning a story to retell. Have children 'tell about' their story, in pairs or groups of three. Encourage them to ask each other questions about the stories. This helps each teller to think more carefully about the story — the characters, setting and action.

Chapter 5

STORY PRESENTATION

I'll tell you a story about Jackanory
And now my story's begun.

Preparing to tell a story is largely a problem-solving process, with certain issues that need to be addressed: the features of the story and the story-teller's interpretation of it. The storyteller needs to be aware of a number of aspects, and the following checklist may be useful.

Checklist for story presentation

1 The story

Is it interesting? The teller must like the story and want to share it with others. A storyteller who feels indifferent about a story will transfer this indifference to the audience.

Is it appropriate? The story needs to be appropriate to the teller's level of experience, as well as to the age and interest level of the audience.

Does it appeal to the senses? Some stories appeal to the ear with their unusual and often onomatopoeic words. For example in the African tale *Why Mosquitoes Buzz in People's Ears* (Aardema, 1975), the iguana goes off *'mek mek mek'* and the python slides *'wasu wusu'* into the rabbit's hole. Other stories, on the other hand, are very visual. Children need to think about their story's appeal to the senses and to work at communicating this to the audience.

Length. The story's length is a consideration for both the teller and the audience. Young children are more able to enjoy and understand fairly short stories, whereas older children have longer attention spans. From the teller's point of view, a long story will mean greater effort in remembering the action and being able to sustain interest in the story.

2 Story structure

Beginning. The opening lines of the story are very important. A shaky start tends to unsettle the audience. Children need to give their story a strong, confident beginning: this will alert the audience to the importance of the story and give the teller the necessary confidence to continue.

Middle. The middle of the story should maintain the plot sequence and not lose direction. The audience should be able to visualise this part of the telling clearly.

End. The end, like the beginning, should be confidently delivered. An ending that is mumbled, rushed or uncertain will leave the audience perplexed. After the story is finished, the teller should remain in position and allow a few seconds' pause. The audience may need time to come out of the story. Feeling comfortable with a few seconds of silence is an important skill to learn. The teller also needs to accept applause without feeling embarrassed. After all, it is probably well earned!

3 The storyteller

Voice. Children need plenty of encouragement to explore the full potential of their voices. Consider the following aspects — expression, enunciation, correct pronunciation of words, tone, volume, effective use of pause and timing.

Face. A teller with an expressive face which reflects the mood (and changes of mood) of the story will help to convey the story more effectively than one who shows the strain of intense concentration. The storyteller has to develop a natural manner and not be over-dramatic as this could detract from the story itself. Of course there are stories which are meant to be exaggerated, but it is important to know how far one can go before turning the story into a farce.

Eye contact. This is essential. Many novice tellers (young and old) tend to tell the story to the floor, the back wall, their feet or the side of the room. When children learn to maintain eye contact with their audience they are indeed giving the story to the audience and their telling will be more confident as a result.

54

Gesture. Gestures can be distracting. Through nervousness, children often scratch their noses, play with their hair and fiddle with their fingers. Videotaping their storytelling is one way of showing them how their unconscious gestures distract. However, videotaping could prove damaging to the child's self-confidence, so make it optional. Positive gestures with the hands and body — turning one's head slowly to indicate the presence of another, pointing a finger in the distance, or rocking slowly back and forth as if on a rocking chair — can add to the characterisation and dramatic impact of the story.

Familiarity with the story. Storytelling is not storyreading, so children should not have notes or a book to help them when they are presenting their story. Storytelling is not like acting where the script has to be word perfect. Storytellers should be so familiar with the story that they feel confident to tell it in their own way, using their own words where necessary.

Posture. Children need to observe how experienced storytellers position themselves when telling a story. Good posture will also aid correct breathing. Children need to look comfortable with their body posture and position, whether they choose to sit or stand or move about.

Warm-up activities

These are a way of 'breaking the ice' and getting children relaxed and into the right frame of mind for storytelling. The following exercises will help make children aware of how their storytelling presentations are affected by voice, posture, breathing and relaxation. Build on these exercises with the children to give more variety.

Voice

Have the children:

- Sing scales — down and up, up and down.

- Try 'vocal fry' — using a simple sentence like 'Help me, sonny', speak like a very old person by vibrating the vocal chords.

- Stress different words in a statement. For example, '*I* said I would'; 'I *said* I would'; 'I said *I* would'; 'I said I *would*'.

- Alter pitch, for example say 'Fee Fi Fo Fum' in the lowest limit of vocal range; in the middle range; then the highest range. Say it as different characters, for example as an old giant without teeth, a sassy witch, an enthusiastic football player.

- Practise shortening and lengthening vowels, for example: 'To whom do you wish to speak?'

- Practise saying a sentence such as 'I said march here on the double' with soft consonants and then with hard consonants.

- Practise changing the shape of the mouth. For example say 'Oh, you are flattering me' with a mouth shaped like a circle; in a fixed grin; with lips barely moving.

- Tell tongue twisters as fast as possible without getting the words in a tangle. Then say each word slowly and precisely.

- Concentrate on change of pace by saying 'I want to sleep' in a slow sleepy voice; in a demanding, loud voice; as an incredulous question; in a definite, no-fuss manner.

Breathing

Correct breathing helps voice control and relaxes the body. Have the children:

- Practise breathing in short, sharp pants.

- Inhale through one nostril and then the other to feel the breath come from the diaphragm.

- Kneel on the floor on all fours. Expel the air from the lungs. Don't breathe in air for a few seconds, then take a deep breath.

Posture

Good posture helps to give the audience a good impression of the story-teller and also helps the storyteller's control of voice and movements. Have the children:

- Stand with the back, shoulders and buttocks touching the wall. Walk feet out a few steps; drop the lower jaw; wait a few seconds, then walk ahead. This exercise gives you an instant lift and great posture.

- Stand with a straight back and legs relaxed with feet slightly apart.

Relaxation

Have the children:

- Lie in a space on the floor, close their eyes and listen to a relaxing piece of music, or help them visualise a peaceful scene by talking through a description of a beach, or a waterfall in a rainforest.

- Imagine they are a candle burning down very slowly.

- Lying in a space on the floor, relax and tense parts of the body one at a time: toes, feet, legs, arms, hands (fists), neck, face.

- Stand in a circle and turn to face the right. Each person then massages the shoulders and neck of the person in front. Then face to the left and massage again.

Working with an audience

Rituals

Rituals are an important part of many of our social interactions. When we go the theatre, a restaurant, a football match, church, we often conform to established rituals. The adherence to the ritual helps to contribute to the sense of the occasion.

Storytelling also has traditional rituals. In many cultures there is a ritual language spoken by the teller to signify that storytelling is about to commence (for example, 'Once upon a time . . .'). Sometimes there is ritual bantering between teller and audience, as in the Caribbean, where the storyteller calls out 'Cric' and if the audience wants to hear the story they will respond with an enthusiastic 'Crac!'

Adult tellers have often incorporated rituals when telling stories to children, as a way of establishing a sense of occasion. In the classroom, the commencement of storytime may be signalled by unrolling a special banner, or having the storyteller sit in a special chair or wear a special storytelling cape. Children can employ some of these rituals or invent their own to help establish a mood of excitement and expectation.

Audience involvement

Storytelling is always a two-way process, because the audience is actively involved in visualising and interpreting the storyteller's words. Some stories lend themselves to more physical audience involvement. For example ritual language in a story can be sung, clapped, chanted or even danced to by the

57

audience. This type of involvement may sometimes be spontaneous; at other times the storyteller can lead the audience into participating.

Encourage children to discover whether their stories lend themselves to audience participation. When props are used to help tell a story, a member of the audience might be invited to come out and hold a puppet or place a felt piece on a board.

The storyteller might like to involve the audience before the story begins by asking them a question which relates to the story. For example one might ask, 'Has any one ever been really scared at night?' as a way of leading into a ghost story; a riddle could be asked as a cryptic way of introducing the main character or theme of the story.

Storytelling to other classes

When children have had experience in telling their stories to their own classmates, they could invite another class to come and hear their stories. This could be a cooperative activity, with children and teacher deciding on the wording and format of a written invitation (desktop publishing skills could be used here) and on the format of the program: who will act as convenor, who will tell the stories and in what order, how to set up the room.

An evening for parents

Once children have had experience telling to other children they should be confident enough to tell to their parents and those of their classmates. Preparations could be similar to those outlined above, perhaps with the inclusion of light refreshments (which the children can also organise). As one to one and a half hours is the maximum time for this type of function, not everyone will perform.

Storytelling in the community

There are many opportunities for storytelling in the community: senior citizens groups, children's wards in the hospital, Scout and Girl Guide clubs, public libraries. In such instances it is preferable to have one story-teller performing for a small group, rather than having each child tell a story, one at a time.

Storytelling on school camps and excursions

Teachers and children can add to the fun and experience of school camps and excursions by telling stories. These oral sessions can often lead into written language activities. For example a visit to a museum exhibition provides an ideal opportunity for sharing stories about the experience. Other written activities can follow, such as responding to the experience with a poem or personal impressions. This type of activity may be more meaningful than filling in a teacher-prepared sheet of questions about the exhibition.

Storytelling festival

This is a true celebration of story. Just as schools often meet at a central location for an interschool sports day or a week-long music camp, why not an opportunity for schools to meet for a day or a week of storytelling?

The purpose of such a gathering is the celebration and sharing of stories, not a competition to determine the best storytellers. There are enormous benefits for children in this type of activity.

Format of a storytelling program

Careful planning needs to go into the format of a storytelling program. Children can learn a lot by being involved in the design of the format. Consideration needs to be given to the following:

- The opening story is important, as it will set the tone for the evening.

- Stories should be sequenced to achieve a balance. For example a long story followed by a short story is often better than two long stories in a row; a serious story followed by a humorous one may bring in a suitable change of mood.

- 'Fillers' (songs, riddles, anecdotes and so on) can be used for a change of pace and style.

- The last story should be carefully considered because it is the one that the audience will leave with. So consider the mood — reflective, happy, sad, frightened?

- The length of the program needs to be tailored to the age and interest level of the audience. Telling to an infant class is quite different from telling to an adult audience, which is different again from telling to a mixed-age audience. Thirty minutes is long enough for preschoolers and Years 1, 2 and 3; older children and an adult audience can usually manage an hour comfortably.

In summary, children need to be given plenty of time to prepare themselves for presenting their stories publicly — whether to their classmates, to others in the school or to community members. The checklist given earlier in this chapter can be used by children when they are critiquing their own performances as well as those of their classmates. A fine balance needs to be maintained so that story preparation does not become drudgery — or worse, a confidence-destroying experience.

Chapter 6

STORYTELLING ACROSS THE CURRICULUM

Captain Cook chased a chook
All around Australia
Lost his pants in the middle of France
And found them in Tasmania.

Captain Cook Chased a Chook (Factor 1988)

Before you read this chapter you may find it useful to review chapter 2, which argued the case for children as storytellers. The purpose now is to show how storytelling can be used by both teachers and children for teaching and learning across the curriculum. Storytelling has a very important function in any language program, but it is also useful in other subject areas.

Learning through storytelling

For centuries teachers have used storytelling to instruct and entertain. Think back to the teachers you enjoyed the most when you were at school: they probably enlivened their lessons with anecdotes and other forms of story. Films such as *Dead Poets Society* and *Stand and Deliver* illustrate how teachers use story in the form of personal anecdotes and analogies to stimulate students' imagination and their desire to learn and understand.

Turner (1988, p. 68) says that 'the world "comes to us" in the shape of stories'. Through story we construct our world and many of us 'make sense' of everyday happenings by sharing our oral narratives. This is especially true for children, as narrative is their main mode of making meaning about the world.

Many skills, attitudes and concepts can be learnt through story. Storytelling can be the effective means by which these are mastered

61

because it uses spoken, not written, language. Storytelling relies on the language that children use and can understand; the language that they bring to school. The combination of the story and the teller's language can establish a rapport which helps children connect with literature. Children relate to a story by drawing on their own language and experiences. Learning takes place when this new experience is accommodated within their existing knowledge.

Many teachers subconsciously use stories in their teaching. This informal type of storytelling forms part of the hidden curriculum. The story told may be intended to discipline, to explain, to entertain, to praise, to warn, to set an example, to reassure — whatever the purpose, it is a spontaneous discourse which the teller embarks on at that moment. For some students the story may provide a temporary distraction from the task at hand; for others it may have some personal significance; others may see it as just another feature of 'teacher talk'. However the teacher or students perceive the story, the fact remains that storytelling in all its many shapes and forms is part of daily life at school.

Storytelling of a more formal and conscious nature can be used for specific instructional purposes. Comprehension skills, both literal and inferential, can be developed through storytelling. The literal level of comprehension is probably the most common asked of children by teachers. Children can be led to identify with a character or the problem in the story, and comprehend the final resolution. Nelson (1989, p. 389) believes that storytelling provides children 'with a perfect opportunity to make that "conceptual leap" into the metaphorical realm'. Furthermore, Nelson's research has shown that children are able to understand metaphor on both a literary and a personal level. After telling children the story of *The Tailor*, Nelson (p. 387) says:

> ... each child knows exactly how the tailor felt, how he loved his treasured gifts, why he was reluctant to throw away any of the gifts he had made himself, and why the button was more than a mere object. They identify with the tailor and realise the significance of the button as an object, a memory, and as a story.

Problem solving is an intrinsic part of storytelling, for both teller and listener. For the teller the problem begins when looking for a story to tell. During the delivery of the story the teller is subconsciously solving the problems associated with reconstructing the story: the language, the story structure, the paralanguage, the responses of the audience (Livo & Rietz 1986). For the listener there are the problems of visualising the story, and predicting and anticipating its events and likely resolution.

Another aspect of storytelling with implications for children's own creative oral and written stories is the notion of intertexuality. Cairney (1990, p. 480) says that intertextuality is the 'process of interpreting one text by means of a previously composed text'. In other words, when children (and adults) come to read, write, or listen to a text, they draw on previous experiences with similar texts to shape their understanding or composition of the new one.

Cairney's research with eighty Year 6 children from New South Wales showed that when children write they often borrow aspects from stories that they have read or heard in the past. These aspects include specific story content, similar plots, character types and genres. Teachers often encourage the use of literature as models for children's own written narratives.

The intertextual nature of children's own storytelling is a relatively uncharted area of academic research. At an informal level of observation it is true to say that children do incorporate into their oral stories many features of language they have heard or read from other sources. The following oral telling of 'Mr Oz' draws on *The Wizard of Oz* (Baum 1969) for part of the story's content and language:

Once there was a little girl called Jane. She was nine. One day she was skipping when she tripped over and fell in a hole. She was in a new land. There falling from the sky was her kitten Bobby. She started walking. Then she saw a mouse. Jane asked 'Why are you crying?' The mouse said 'The bad witch of the West is chasing me'. So they all ran. After a while they met a bunny. They told the bunny that the witch was chasing them. So the bunny said he would run with them. — Kimberley, aged 8

By encouraging more storytelling in our classrooms, we help children to develop and extend their use of language, and their knowledge about language and its effects on communication. The range and diversity of the storytelling experiences we offer will help also to broaden their world view.

Language education: Implications for storytelling

The *P–10 Language Education Framework* document (Queensland Dept of Education 1989, p. 24) states the importance of practical application of the language curricula:

Language curricula should involve children in using language in a variety of interesting and challenging activities which serve important purposes for

*them. Since children learn best by 'doing', and 'doing' provides the best
context for 'reflecting on' or 'learning about' language, inductive learning
approaches should predominate.*

Storytelling not only provides the variety and the challenge of active
language activities; it is also an inductive means of teaching and learning.

Oral language objectives

Students will:

- Develop competence and confidence in communicating to peers and
  teacher (and others) their ideas, attitudes and experiences, both literary
  and personal.

- Employ successfully the conventions of oral language such as intona-
  tion, pitch, stress, juncture; and articulate clearly.

- Use acquired vocabulary (words, phrases and other language patterns
  from story sources) in retelling other stories.

- Take on the viewpoint of the author and identify with the main character, thus giving a feeling of conviction and sense of authority to the
  retelling.

Listening objectives

Students will:

- Develop respect for other storytellers and give them support in their
  efforts by being good listeners.

- Learn to listen for detail (of language and content) and overall meaning.

- Learn to discriminate and evaluate according to the strengths and weaknesses of a range of story genres and storytelling styles (Livo & Rietz
  1986).

- Be able to evaluate their own effectiveness as listeners (Livo & Rietz
  1986).

Written language objectives

Students will:

- Develop knowledge of a framework for understanding texts and be able
  to draw on this framework when composing written narratives.

- Be able to incorporate language patterns and conventions of other stories into their personal creative stories.
- Bring to their personal writing a background experience and general knowledge of world beliefs, values, and relationships.

Reading objectives

Students will:

- Develop a repertoire of organisational strategies (prediction and hypothesising skills) for handling reading.
- Discover a wide range of literary genres in searching for a story to retell and following up on stories heard.
- See reading as pleasurable and purposeful.
- Develop a sense of critical awareness and discrimination based on personal preference and literary quality.

Other curriculum areas will adapt the above objectives to their own specific content.

Practical activities across the curriculum

A word of caution must be given at this point: it is important that, in our enthusiasm to incorporate storytelling into our curriculum, we do not lose sight of our purpose. Storytelling is a useful and important teaching and learning strategy and while many concepts, skills and attitudes may be best explained or understood through story there will be many others that are best dealt with in other ways. The integrity of the story should not be sacrificed for the sake of teaching specifics.

Language education

Life stories

Ask children to imagine they are researching the biography of someone in their class. Compile a list of questions which the children feel would be the appropriate ones to ask. Individually, children choose questions from the list and interview a classmate (not a close friend). Once the information is recorded the interviewer then compiles the biography to share with the class. A class book of the children's life stories (with photographs) can be compiled.

Vocabulary file

Drawing on stories they have heard or read, children collect unusual and interesting words and their meanings, write these on cards and file them in a class dictionary box. Encourage children to refer to the file when writing.

Travel advertisements

Children can design and write travel advertisements for places encountered in stories, for example the giant's castle in *Jack and the Beanstalk* (Stobbs 1965), the gingerbread house in *Hansel and Gretel* (Grimm & Grimm 1981), the cottage in *Goldilocks and the Three Bears* (Garrity 1987). They can compile an information sheet for each location, 'available on request' and including information on airfares, accommodation, facilities, rules and so on. This activity helps children to visualise setting, by imagining locations in such detail that they can communicate them clearly to others.

Tall tales

Collect tall tales both from oral and written sources: newspaper stories, Speewah tales (Edwards 1980), fishing stories and so on. Children can create their own tall tales for a storytelling competition.

Rewrites

Have the children rewrite a folktale in some other form, for example in a modern setting or as a Readers Theatre script, a poem, radio broadcast or newspaper article. Stories like *Jim and the Beanstalk* (Briggs 1970), *Prince Cinders* (Cole 1987) and *Princess Smartypants* (Cole 1986) are good examples of modern fairytales.

Poem to prose

Find a poem for children to rewrite as prose. Ballads work very well because they usually have a strong storyline; or try more bizarre poems such as those found in the following collections:

Songs for My Dog and Other People (Fatchen 1980)
You Can't Catch Me! (Rosen, M. 1981)

Sky in the Pie (McGough 1983)
Where the Sidewalk Ends (Silverstein 1974)

Vocal jazz

Vocal jazz, according to Barton (1986, p. 69), is 'another method of creating stories [which] focuses on the sounds and rhythms of words hooked together thematically'. Try asking children to name breakfast cereals. List these on the board, then ask children to explore ways of saying the words, for example:

> *Rice Bubble-bubble-bubble*
> *Coco Pops! Coco Pops!*
> *Cooorrrnnn Flakes! Cooorrrnnn Flakes!*

Now ask children to work in groups and decide on a specific story context (a school camp, breakfast in the bush).

Divide the class into groups and have them decide how they are going to tell their story, incorporating and performing their vocal jazz. Within each group, certain words or groups of words can be spoken individually, in pairs, in unison and so on.

Variation. Try using *Animalia* (Base 1986) as the basis for vocal improvisation. Children could make up lists of their favourite words either from the text or the illustrations and rearrange them to make interesting sound and word combinations.

Shared storytelling

Write four words on the board, for example *car, friend, $10, shoe*. In groups, children make up a story incorporating these words. Groups share their stories, with each person in the group telling part of the story.

Variation. Instead of words, use pictures for this activity.

Group retellings

Have groups retell a story which has just been read to them. They can be free to embellish or change the story according to the group's wishes.

Photographs

Select a number of photographs, both black and white and colour, preferably covering a wide timespan. Avoid any photographs in which you appear, as anonymity is important.

Place the photographs on tables and invite groups to browse and select one photograph which brings back a memory, a story or a scene from their own lives. Have them share their personal stories. (Morgan & Rinvolucri 1983.)

Point of view

Give the children two characters (e.g. a teacher, a child) and a word (e.g. *money*). Children write a one-paragraph story which involves all three elements, but told from one point of view only. The stories must be written within a certain time, say fifteen minutes. Collect the stories and redistribute them so that everyone receives someone else's story. Then set another time limit for everyone to rewrite the story from the other character's point of view. Share the finished stories.

Arts education

Music

Use non-story resources such as tongue twisters, riddles, chants and rhymes and try setting them to music. (A music specialist could help with this activity.) Some simple examples are contained in the following anthologies:

Silly Verse for Kids (Milligan 1968)
What Do You Feed Your Donkey On? (O'Hare 1978)
Tomie de Paola's Mother Goose (de Paola 1985)

The recording *Playmates with Mike and Michelle* (ABC 1983) has some examples of rhymes set to song.

Drama games

'Drama games form part of the cultural heritage of all people' (Barton 1986, p. 99). These games are often played when people get together at a celebration of some kind, to demonstrate a unity of purpose and provide a ritualised play where people can share and enjoy each other's company. Children can add gestures and create new movements to accompany rhymes. *Raps and Rhymes* (Hill 1990) gives some good examples. *Tell Me Another* (Barton 1986) also details several games.

Tableaus

Children can create tableaus or 'still photographs' of scenes from a story as it is being told. Experiment with different scenes before the story is told and performed: for example the witch calling up to Rapunzel in the tower (tableau 1); Rapunzel letting down her hair (tableau 2); and the Prince climbing the hair (tableau 3). Emphasise that the tableaus are non-verbal, frozen states.

Faces in the crowd

Show the children magazine photographs of groups of people, then discuss: Who could these people be? Where are they? What do they do for a living? — and so on. Once the children feel comfortable with a photograph they can role-play the people in a story context, for example as observers of the street parade in *The Emperor's New Clothes* (Andersen 1973) or guests at the ball in *Cinderella* (Perrault 1978). A roving reporter can do 'on the spot' interviews.

Paint, draw, model

Encourage children to create paintings, drawings or models of scenes, settings or characters from a story, using a wide selection of materials.

Puppets

Children can make puppets and rehearse telling a story using the puppets. This activity requires a lot of work with puppets before the story can be retold successfully.

Feelings: Non-verbal communication

After hearing a story, children interpret the different characters' feelings using only gestures and facial expressions.

Social education

Stories from around the world

Children find and tell stories from different countries. Discussion may focus on lifestyles, housing, food, customs and rituals. Stories and their geographical locations can be displayed on a large map on the wall. This activity gives children a sense of the universality of stories.

Religious stories

Religious beliefs and rituals can be understood through stories from different cultures. Creation myths (e.g. Stewart 1987) and Bible stories can be used to demonstrate different peoples' religious beliefs and worship and their explanations for the creation of the universe. Philosophical differences can be understood better (and, hopefully, respected) in this context. Members from the community may be invited to share their stories.

Community stories

Many stories are concerned with the individual as a member of society, and relationships between the community and the family. Stories from different cultures can be used for comparing and discussing societal rules, laws, customs and roles. Punishment for breaking rules or disrupting the natural order is a common theme in many tales. For example 'How Kwaku Anansi was Punished for His Bad Manners' (Appiah 1987) looks at tolerance and respect for others. Telling and sharing these stories also helps children to see life from someone else's point of view.

Active female heroes and role-breaking males also feature in several tales and these are important to balance those stories which stereotype male and female roles. Sharing these traditional stories helps pave the way for modern comparisons and discussions. Useful collections include:

East of the Sun and West of the Moon (Asbjornsen & Moe 1963)
The Woman in the Moon and Other Tales of Forgotten Heroines (Riordan 1984)
'Baba Yaga's Daughter' (*Stories Round the World*, 1990).

Fables

Fables are useful for helping children understand values, and human motives and behaviour. For example *The Rich Man and the Shoemaker* (La Fontaine 1965) is a good example of how riches do not necessarily bring peace and contentment — a sobering thought in these get-rich-quick days of lotteries and scratch-it cards.

Local history

Children can interview long-time residents in their local area and record their stories about life in earlier times and changes to the local community. These stories can be retold by the children and shared with other children and adults.

Australian history

Children could research the people who shaped Australia's past: the original inhabitants, explorers, convicts, governors, housemaids, landowners, storekeepers, goldminers and so on. They could then tell their stories in role. Contemporary adventurers and history-makers (Kay Cottee, Dick Smith) can also be explored in a similar way. This approach to history is often more interesting and results in more purposeful learning than recording accounts in a solely expository style.

Family stories

Family photograph albums can be a good source for family stories and anecdotes. Encourage children to explore this idea with their families, but be aware that this may be a touchy area for some children.

Mathematics and science education

Stories are a valuable means for learning maths and science as they can actively involve students in the process of problem solving and making connections between stories and facts.

Number stories

Share stories which have a number pattern (see chapter 4 for some examples) and encourage children to tell their own number pattern stories.
   The Five Chinese Brothers (Bishop 1938) and *Six Foolish Fishermen* (Elkin 1958) can be told to introduce the concept of one-to-one correspondence and basic counting.

Riddles

Riddles encourage problem solving and divergent thinking skills. Children will have a ready source of their own riddles which can be shared; or explore stories which contain riddles, such as 'The Riddles' in *World Tales* (Shah 1979).

The solar system

Share Greek and Roman myths about the deities after whom the planets were named, as a way of introducing children to a study of the solar system. For example tell the story of the Roman god Mars and his relationship with his two sons to explain the planet and its moons (Martin & Miller 1988).

Weather lore

According to Martin & Miller (1989, p. 256), 'Weather lore invites children to look at the world more carefully and, thereby, to ascertain the extent to which their observations are accurately reflected in the lore'. Some common weather lore:

> *Red sky in the morning, sailor's warning; Red sky at night, sailor's delight. Birds flying high, the weather will be dry; Birds flying near the ground, soon you'll hear the thunder's sound.*

Through observation and recording, children can test the truth of these sayings. They could also observe how human behaviour is affected by the weather.

Famous scientists

Ask children to research famous scientists of the past (Aristotle, Copernicus, Kepler, Galileo, Newton, Curie, Einstein) and tell how their observations, questioning and experiments changed the scientific thinking of their time.

Using books, newspapers, science programs, current affairs and news programs on television and radio, children can also research contemporary scientists and tell their stories.

Heat

Introduce the idea of heat as a form of energy through stories about the 'hot' gods — Prometheus, Zeus, Phaeton, Hephaestus. Children can discuss the relationship between fire and power, and fire as the giver and destroyer of life.

Tell stories about the discovery of steam as a source of energy to explain how heat is used to change water to steam. Children can conduct similar experiments to discover this phenomenon for themselves (Egan 1986).

To conclude: storytelling has an important place not only in the language program, but also in other curriculum areas. Oral stories have a way of helping children make meanings, see associations and form analogous relationships in their thinking. Having children tell stories not only enhances listening and speaking skills, but also provides a vehicle for demonstrating their comprehension.

Chapter 7

WHERE TO FROM HERE?

Three apples fell from heaven.
One for the teller,
One for the listener,
And one for all the peoples of the world.

Armenian ritual closing

This book started with 'Beginnings', but there is no ending. Storytelling has been with us since the beginning of humankind and it will continue for as long as we exist on this earth.

Schools and schooling have always experienced changes, and no doubt changes will continue to be made — to curricula, teaching strategies, educational jargon and our theories about children's learning. While storytelling has seen a revival of interest in schools over recent years, it has the potential to survive and elude the ephemerality of passing fads. Its survival depends partly on teachers' commitment to its preservation. Many students will continue to tell their stories, whether teachers continue to develop formal storytelling courses or not. As for those students who do not come from households which value the exchanges of storytelling in its many different forms, teachers can ensure that they are not deprived of their rightful inheritance.

Evaluation: Handle with care

Though this book offers numerous suggestions for encouraging children to take on the role of storyteller, it is not the intention that teachers regard storytelling as another new curriculum to be taught and tested. Many high schools offer storytelling electives as part of their English curriculum, and in these cases formal evaluation seems necessary. One hopes that the evaluation of students' storytelling, at whatever level in the school, is seen as a way of improving existing skills and not as a way of sorting out the 'failures'. If we destroy children's confidence and self-esteem, then they will see storytelling as something they cannot do. Sadly this has happened to many children who 'learnt' from a very young age that they were not good at reading. This kind of self-fulfilling prophecy should be avoided at all costs.

Aims of a storytelling program

The overarching aim of any storytelling program must be to develop individuals' confidence in their ability to use oral language. I have seen adults who are too frightened to sing with family or friends for fear of ridicule. We don't want children to feel that they cannot share with their family and friends the songs of their experiences.

Children's writing has been grouped into three broad purposes: personal, literary and public. Storytelling can also serve these same broad purposes. It begins with stories which stem from personal experiences. To this personal range can be added stories retold from literary sources. The public side of storytelling comes whenever stories are shared with a group. This is also an important part of the storytelling process because the teller has a responsibility to share stories and keep alive the oral tradition of our cultural heritage.

Storytelling for public performance is something many people enjoy, but for others it can be an excruciating experience. Some children will relish the opportunity to tell their stories to an audience; some will need encouragement to meet the challenge; others will regard it as an anathema. Respect the individual's decision, and offer support and encouragement for all. Remember, the performance is not the end product!

What the children say

Perhaps it is fitting to conclude with some comments from students I have worked with in the writing of *Children as Storytellers*.

I like storytelling. It's nice when you gather round with your friends and tell each other different stories. The storyteller can use facial expressions and movement. I told 'The Yellow Ribbon' to my brother and he told it to all his friends. — Biljana, aged 12

Storytelling is really good because when you're up there in the chair and telling to an audience it gives you confidence in yourself. — Sean, aged 12

I like doing the storyboards. They help you revise it before you tell it and it helps the story to stick in your memory better. — Joshua, aged 12

Storytelling describes a story better than just reading a story because you can add your own descriptive words. — Kylie, aged 12

I like storytelling because you learn how to read well and you expand your vocabulary. — Lisa, aged 12

Storytelling is good because you get to improve your oral expression and it boosts up your confidence. It's fun and exciting. — Jade, aged 12

I like storytelling because you can get the audience involved in it. They can join in at different parts. — Andrew, aged 12

With storytelling there are bits added that aren't in the story. — Robert, aged 11

Storytelling is more enjoyable than having a story read to you. You never feel bored, you are just waiting for the next part. — Tamara, aged 12

It's different from what I thought it would be. I thought it would be real boring but it's good when you get started. It's good telling to little kids than older kids. I enjoyed it. — Matt, aged 12

You learn lots of new stories to tell your friends. I told my friends the one about 'The Gunny Wolf' and they thought it was okay. — Dwayne, aged 11

After you've done storytelling and when you have to get up and talk in front of the class it was easier. — Tamie, aged 12

Storytelling is excellent. You tell stories and you can make people laugh. — Nathan, aged 11

When you tell a really good story and you've got the audience's attention you feel really great because you know they're not bored. You can make the characters come to life. — Shane, aged 12

Storytelling is really good. It gets you in. It's fun all round. — Michael, aged 13

When you tell a story in your own words you can make it more exciting, more scary or whatever. — Craig, aged 12

I think it is good when a storyteller has got a good story to tell. When someone has a hopeless, boring story it's not very good. When you are out in the bush around a fire it's good to tell stories. — Ben, aged 13

When you're storytelling you can use expressions, with your body and face. You can make people feel scared or like a lovely day in the park. You have to put a lot of hard work into it, into researching and putting your story into your own words, and then you've got to have the guts to get up there and tell your story. — Lex, aged 12

REFERENCES

(Where available, U.S. publishing details have been listed.)

Aardema, V. (1978), *Why Mosquitoes Buzz in People's Ears: A West African Tale*, Dial.

Andersen, Hans Christian (1972), *The Ugly Duckling*, Blackie.

———(1973), *The Emperor's New Clothes*, Hamish Hamilton.

Appiah, P. (1989), *Tales of an Ashanti Father*, Beacon Press.

Arbuthnot, M. Hill (1961), *Time for Fairy Tales Old and New*, Scott Foresman.

Asbjornsen, P. C. & Moe, T. E. (1963), *East of the Sun and West of the Moon*, Macmillan.

Baillie, A. (1984), *Adrift*, Nelson.

Barton, B. (1986), *Tell Me Another*, Heinemann.

Base, G. (1987), *Animalia*, Abrams.

Bauer, Caroline Feller (1977), *Handbook for Storytellers*, American Library Association.

Baum, L. F. (1969), *The Wizard of Oz*, ill. P. Granger, Collins.

Berger, P. & Luckmann, T. (1967), *The Social Construction of Reality—A Treatise in the Sociology of Knowledge*, Doubleday.

Bishop, C. (1989), *The Five Chinese Brothers*, Putnam.

Briggs, Raymond, (1989), *Jim and the Beanstalk*, Putnam.

Britton, J. (1979), *Language and Learning*, Penguin.

Brown, M. (1986), *Stone Soup: An Old Tale*, Macmillan.

Caimey, T. (1990), 'Intertexuality: Infectious Echoes from the Past', *The Reading Teacher*, March, vol. 43, no. 7, pp. 478-84.

Chukovsky, K. (1965), *From Two to Five*, University of California.

Cole, B. (1987), *Princess Smartypants*, Putnam.

———(1988), *Prince Cinders*, Putnam.

Crosson, V. & Stailey, J. (1988), *Spinning Stories: An Introduction to Storytelling Skills*, Texas State Library.

Davis, Z. & McPherson, M. (1989), 'Story Map Instruction: A Road Map for Reading Comprehension', *The Reading Teacher*, December, pp. 232-40.

de Paola, T. (1979), *Strega Nona*, Simon & Schuster.

———(1985), *Tomie de Paola's Mother Goose*, Putnam.

Dwyer, E. (1988), A Pleasant Journey into Classroom Storytelling, Paper presented at Tennessee Reading Association Conference.

Edwards, P. (1980), *Crooked Mick of Speewah*, Reed.

Egan, K. (1989), *Teaching as Storytelling*, University of Chicago.

Elkin, B. (1958), *Six Foolish Fishermen*, Brockhampton.

Erasmus, C. Chambers (1989), 'Ways with Stories: Listening to the Stories Aboriginal People Tell', *Language Arts*, March, vol. 66, no. 3, pp. 267-75.

Factor, J. (1988), *Captain Cook Chased a Chook: Children's Folklore in Australia*, Penguin.

Fatchen, M. (1980), *Songs for My Dog and Other People*, Puffin, Penguin.

Ferguson, V. & Durkin, P. (1989), *Rotten Apples: Top Stories to Read and Tell*, Nelson.

Fox, M. (1985), *Wilfrid Gordon McDonald Partridge*, Kane Miller.

Frye, N. (1964), *The Educated Imagination*, Indiana University.

Galdone, Paul (1987), *The Monkey and the Crocodile: A Jakata Tale from India*, Ticknor & Fields.

Garnett, K. (1986), 'Telling Tales: Narratives and Learning—Disabled Children', *Topics in Language Discourse*, March, vol. 6, no. 2, pp. 44-52.

Garrity, Linda (1987), *The Gingerbread Guide*, Scott, Foresman.

Gilbert, P. (1989), *Gender, Literacy and the Classroom*, Australian Reading Association.

Grimm, Jacob & Grimm, Wilhelm (1960), *Rapunzel*, ill. Felix Hoffman, Oxford University.

———(1968), *The Bremen Town Musicians*, McGraw-Hill.

———(1970), *The Fisherman and His Wife*, ill. Katrin Brandt, Bodley Head.

———(1975a), *Snow White and the Seven Dwarfs*, ill. Otto S. Svend, Pelham.

———(1975b), *Hans in Luck*, ill. Felix Hoffman, Oxford University.

———(1977), *The Wolf and the Seven Little Kids*, ill. Otto S. Svend, Pelham.

———(1981), *Hansel and Gretel*, ill. Susan Jeffers, Hamish Hamilton.

Haley, Gail (1988), *A Story, a Story*, Macmillan.

Hallworth, Grace (1978), *Listen to this Story: Tales from the West Indies*, Magnet.

Haviland, V. (1969), *Favourite Fairy Tales Told in Japan*, Bodley Head.

Hill, S. (1990), *Raps and Rhymes*, Eleanor Curtain.

Hobday, Sr Maria Jose (1979) 'Strung Memories', *Parabola*, vol. iv, no. 4, pp. 4–11.

Huck, C., Hepler, S. & Hickman, J. (1987), *Children's Literature in the Elementary School*, Holt Rinehart & Winston.

Ireson, Barbara (1963), *The Gingerbread Man*, Faber & Faber.

Johnson, D. (1981), 'Storytelling to the Elderly' Wilson Library Bulletin, vol. 55, no. 8, pp. 593-5.

Kent, J. (1984), *The Fat Cat, a Danish Folktale*, Puffin, Penguin Books.

King, M. & McKenzie, M. (1988), 'Research Currents: Literary Discourse from the Child's Perspective' *Language Arts*, vol. 65, no. 3, pp. 304-13.

Kraska, E. (1979), *Toys and Tales from Grandmother's Attic*, Houghton Mifflin.

La Fontaine, J. (1965), *The Rich Man and the Shoemaker*, ill. Brian Wildsmith, Oxford University.

———(1966), *The Hare and the Tortoise*, ill. Brian Wildsmith, Oxford University.

Lionni, L. (1987), *Frederick*, Knopf.

———(1975), *Tico and the Golden Wings*, Knopf.

Livo, N. & Rietz, S. (1986), *Storytelling Process and Practice*, Libraries Unlimited.

McDermott, G. (1974), *The Magic Tree*, Kestrel.

MacDonald, Margaret Read (1986), *Twenty Tellable Tales*, Wilson.

McGough, R. (1983), *Sky in the Pie*, Kestrel.

McNamee, G., McLean, J., Cooper, P. & Kerwin, S. (1985), 'Cognition and Effect in Early Literacy Development', *Early Child Development and Care*, no. 20, pp. 229–44.

Martin, K. & Miller, E. (1988), 'Storytelling and Science', *Language Arts*, vol. 65, no. 3, pp. 255–9.

Mayne, William, ed. (1972), *A Book of Giants*, Puffin, Penguin Books.

Merriam, E. (1968), *Epaminondas*, Follett.

Milligan, S. (1968), *Silly Verse for Kids*, Penguin.

Morgan, J. & Rinvolucri, M. (1984), *Once Upon a Time: Using Stories in the Language Classroom*, Cambridge University Press.

Morimoto, J. (1983), *The White Crane*, Collins.

Nelson, O. (1989), 'Storytelling: Language Experience for Meaning Making', *The Reading Teacher*, vol. 42, no. 6, pp. 380–90.

Nielson, J. & Nielson, K. (1969), *The Wishing Pearl and Other Tales of Vietnam*, Harvey.

Nessel, D. (1984), 'Storytelling in the Reading Program', *The Reading Teacher*, vol. 38, no. 1, pp. 378–90.

Norman, D. (1976), *Memory and Attention*, Wiley.

O'Hare, C. (1978), *What Do You Feed Your Donkey On? Rhymes from a Belfast Childhood*, Collins.

Peck, Jackie (1989), 'Using Storytelling to Promote Language and Literacy Development', *The Reading Teacher*, vol. 43, no. 2, November, pp. 138–41.

Peppe, R. (1979), *Three Little Pigs*, Kestrel/Penguin.

Perrault, C. (1978), *Cinderella*, ill. Otto S. Svend, Pelham.

Playmates with Mike and Michelle (1983), ABC Records.

Potter, Beatrix (1986), *The Tale of Mr Tod*, Frederick Warne.

Queensland Department of Education (1989), *P-10 Language Education Framework*, Department of Education, Queensland.

Reed, Barbara (1987), 'Storytelling: What It Can Teach', *School Library Journal*, vol. 34, no. 2, October, pp. 35–9.

Riordan, J. (1985), *The Woman In the Moon and Other Tales of Forgotten Heroines*, Dial.

Rosen, B. (1988), *And None of It Was Nonsense*, Heinemann.

Rosen, M. (1981), *You Can't Catch Me*, Deutsch.

Ross, T. (1986), *Foxy Fables*, Dial.

Sakade, F., ed. (1964), *Urashimo Taro and other Japanese Children's Stories*, Tuttle.

Sawyer, R. (1977), *The Way of the Storyteller*, Viking Penguin.

Sawyer, W. (1987), 'Literature and Literacy: A Review of Research', *Language Arts*, vol. 64, no. 1, pp. 33–9.

Saxby, M. (1990), *The Great Deed of Superheroes*, P. Bedrick.

———(1990), *Tales of Heroic Women*, Millennium.

Schwartz, M. (1987), 'Connecting to Language through Story', *Language Arts*, 64, 6, 603–10.

Shah, Idries (1979), *World Tales*, Harcourt Brace Jovanovich.

Silverstein, S. (1974), *Where the Sidewalk Ends*, HarperCollins.

Spender, Dale (1978), 'The Facts of Life: Sex Differentiated Knowledge in the English Classroom and the School', *English in Education*, vol. 12, no. 3, pp. 1–9.

Stewart, M. (1987), *Creation Myths*, ill. Graeme Base, Macmillan.

Stobbs, W. (1965), *Jack and the Beanstalk*, Constable.

Stories Round the World (1990), Hodder & Stoughton.

Tolstoy, A. (1968), *The Great Big Enormous Turnip*, Heinemann.

Tough, J. (1974), *Talking, Thinking, Growing: Language with the Young Child*, Schocken Books.

Turner, G. (1988), *Film as Social Practice*, Routledge.

Underhill, Liz (1987), *This is the House that Jack Built*, Methuen.

Vygotsky, L. S. (1986), *Thought and Language*, MIT.

Wannan, B. (1974), *Legendary Australians*, Rigby.

White, Anne Terry (1964), *Myths and Legends*, Hamlyn.

Wilson, D. H. (1986), *There's a Wolf in my Pudding*, Dent.

Wolkstein, D. (1987), *The Magic Orange Tree and Other Haitian Folktales*, Schocken.

Yolen, Jane (1981), *Touch Magic*, Putnam.

Zipes, J. (1986), *Don't Bet on the Prince: Contemporary Feminist Fairy Tales in North America and England*, Routledge, Chapman & Hall.

RESOURCES FOR TEACHERS
AND CHILDREN

(Where available, U.S. publishing details have been listed.)

The lists contained here are by no means exhaustive. They represent those resources which I have found to be very useful for storytelling.

Teacher reference

Baker, A. & Greene, E. (1987), *Storytelling: Art and Technique*, Bowker.

Barton, B. (1986), *Tell Me Another*, Heinemann.

Bauer, Caroline Feller (1977), *Handbook for Storytellers*, American Library Association.

———(1983), *This Way to Books*, Wilson.

Bishop, Rita (1988), *Inside Stories*, Ashton Scholastic.

Champlin, C. & Renfro, N. (1985), *Storytelling with Puppets*, American Library Association.

Colwell, E. (1980), *Storytelling*, Bodley Head.

Fox, M. (1980), *Thereby Hangs a Tale: A Storytelling How To*, Sturt College of Advanced Education.

———(1984), *How to Teach Drama to Infants (Without Really Crying!)*, Ashton Scholastic.

Garrity, Linda (1987), *The Gingerbread Guide*, Scott, Foresman.

Griffin, Barbara Budge (1989), *Book One: Students as Storytellers—The Long and the Short of Learning a Story; Book Two: Student StoryFest—How to Organise a Storytelling Festival; Book Three: Storyteller's Journal*, Barbara Budge Griffin, 10 South Keeneway Drive, Medford, Oregon 97504, USA

Irving, J. (1987), *Glad Rags: Stories and Activities Featuring Clothes for Children*, Libraries Unlimited.

Livo, N. & Rietz, S. (1986), *Storytelling Process and Practice*, Libraries Unlimited.

———(1987), *Storytelling Activities*, Libraries Unlimited.

MacDonald, Margaret Read (1982), *The Storyteller's Sourcebook: A Subject, Title and Motif Index to Folklore Collections for Children*, Gale Research Company.

Mallan, Kerry, ed. (1990), *Telling Tales: A Sourcebook of Storytelling Ideas*, Queensland University of Technology.

Morgan, J. & Rinvolucri, M. (1984), *Once Upon a Time: Using Stories in the Language Classroom*, Cambridge University.

Pellowski, A. (1977), *The World Of Storytelling*, Wilson.

————(1984), *The Story Vine: A Source Book of Unusual and Easy-To-Tell Stories from around the World*, Macmillan. (A good reference for teachers and older student tellers. Offers stories and props—sandbox, string, nesting dolls.)

————(1987), *The Family Storytelling Handbook*, Macmillan.

Rosen, B. (1988), *And None of It Was Nonsense*, Heinemann.

Saxby, Maurice, ed. (1979), *Through Folklore to Literature*, International Board on Books for Young People, Australia.

Schimmel, N. (1987), *Just Enough To Make a Story*, 2nd edn, Sisters Choice.

Yolen, J. (1981), *Touch Magic*, Putnam.

Good story sources for children and teachers

Aardema, Verna (1979), *The Riddle of the Drum*, Four Winds. (A cumulative story from Mexico which has potential for audience participation in the chanting of the rhythmical refrain.)

Anderson, Robin (1979), *Sinabouda Lily: a folk tale from Papua New Guinea*, Oxford University.

Appiah, Peggy (1989), *Tales of an Ashanti Father*, Beacon. (A paperback collection of reasonably short stories from the Ashanti people.)

Asbjornsen, P. C. & Moe, T. E. (1963), *East of the Sun and West of the Moon*, Macmillan.

Backer, Carol (1972), *King Midas and the Golden Touch*, Franklin Watts. (The story of the mythical king who longed that everything he touched should turn gold. His wish is granted, with horrifying results.)

Bailey, J., McLeish, K. & Spearman, D. (1981), *Gods and Men: Myths and Legends from the World's Religions*, Oxford University. (A collection from different religions and countries. Includes creation myths, good and evil characters, heroes and prophets.)

Brown, Marcia (1989), *Once a Mouse*, Macmillan. (An Indian story which warns that we must not forget our humble beginnings if we grow big and powerful.)

Corrin, Sara & Corrin, Stephen, eds (1990), *A Time to Laugh*, Faber & Faber. (A collection of traditional and contemporary stories from many countries. All are funny.)

de Paola, Tomie (1979), *Strega Nona*, Simon & Schuster. (Picture book version of how Foolish Anthony learns not to tamper with magic.)

Dickinson, Peter (1980), *City of Gold and Other Stories from the Old Testament*, ill. Michael Foreman, Victor Gollancz. (Creative retellings of thirty-three Bible stories, given voice in the oral rather than the written tradition.)

Downing, Charles (1964), *Tales of the Hodja*, Oxford University. (Delightful stories about Nasreddin Hodja, whose honorary title enables him to perform many different roles in society. All stories are short and many contain humour.)

Ferguson, Virginia & Durkin, Peter (1989), *Rotten Apples: Top Stories to Read and Tell*, Nelson. (A very useful collection of many popular stories for children, and a valuable resource for beginner storytellers.)

Finlay, Winifred (1974), *Cap O' Rushes and Other Folk Tales*, Harvey.

Fritz, Jean (1982), *The Good Giant and the Bad Pukwudgies*, ill. Tomie de Paola, Putnam. (A humorous story which has its origins in the tales told by the Wampanoag tribe of the Algonquin Indians. The story explains how certain landforms were created and gives explanations for such present-day phenomena as fog and annoying mosquitoes.)

Godfrey, John (1963), *The Blind Men and the Elephant*, Saxe. (Six blind men try to describe an elephant by only feeling one part of its body.)

Grimm, Jacob & Grimm, Wilhelm (1970), *The Fisherman and His Wife*, ill. Katrin Brandt, Bodley Head. (A story which shows that greed does not bring happiness.)

Haley, Gail (1988), *A Story, a Story*, Macmillan. (Ananse accomplishes three impossible tasks in order to win the stories from Nyame the Sky God.)

Hallworth, Grace (1978), *Listen to this Story: Tales from the West Indies*, Magnet. (Humorous retellings of West Indian folktales featuring familiar characters like Brer Rabbit.)

Haviland, V. (1959), *Favourite Fairy Tales Told in England*, Bodley Head. (One of many in a series from other countries. Simple, yet well told.)

Hewitt, Anita (1961), *The Tale of the Turnip*, Bodley Head. (An old man plants and grows an enormous turnip. He enlists the help of his wife, grandchildren and several animals to help pull it up.)

Hill, Susan (1990), *Raps and Rhymes*, Eleanor Curtain. (A collection of chants, action rhymes and raps with instructions for clapping and clicking to establish the rhythm and beat.)

Ingram, Anne Bower, ed. (1974), *Too True: Australian Tall Tales*, Collins. (A good collection of Australian tall tales.)

Ireson, Barbara (1963), *The Gingerbread Man*, Faber & Faber. (A cumulative story suitable for young children.)

Jacobs, Joseph (1990), *English Fairy Tales*, Puffin.

Jaffrey, Madhur (1985), *Seasons of Splendour: Tales, Myths and Legends of India*, Hodder & Stoughton. (An excellent collection of tales from Indian mythology and the author's own family tales. Stories are well suited to oral retelling.)

Jarl, Moonie [Wilf Reeves] (1964), *Legends of Moonie Jarl*, Jacaranda.

Johnson, Jane (1985), *A Book of Nursery Riddles*, Houghton Mifflin. (Fifteen riddles which could prove a challenge for all ages.)

Kent, Jack (1972), *The Fat Cat, a Danish Folktale*, Scholastic. (Cumulative tale which tells of a cat's eating binge.)

King, Karen (1985), *Oranges and Lemons*, Oxford University Press. (A collection of singing games and action rhymes with music. Very suitable as storytelling "fillers" for young children.)

Kipling, Rudyard (1912), *Just So Stories*, Doubleday. (These stories are best left to experienced storytellers as many would find the literary style difficult.)

Lobel, Arnold (1980), *Fables*, Harper Collins. (Lobel has written original fables featuring animals.)

Lofts, Pamela (1985), *The Echidna and the Shade Tree*, Slawson. (Tells how the echidna got its spines.)

Logne, Christopher, comp. (1987), *The Children's Book of Children's Rhymes*, Batsford. (A wonderful collection of children's rhymes, skipping games and playground chants. Good source for "fillers" in storytelling programs.)

McDermott, Gerald (1991), *Flecha al Sol*, Viking. (Picture book version of Icarus and Daedalus. Although the illustrations tell of Icarus' death, it is left to the storyteller to describe the fall.)

MacDonald, Fiona (1980), *Little Bird I Have Heard*, Kaye & Ward. (Collection of bird stories from many countries. All stories are short and easy to tell.)

MacDonald, Margaret Read (1986), *Twenty Tellable Tales*, Wilson. (Twenty very tellable tales with notes on ways to tell them. The format of each tale suggests pauses and emphasis on words and phrases. An excellent source for beginners.)

Manning-Sanders, Ruth (1963), *A Book of Giants*, Dutton.

———(1973), *The Book of Ghosts and Goblins*, Dutton.

———(1978), *Old Witch Boneyleg*, Angus & Robertson. (Thirteen folktales and fairytales from around the world which will appeal to children.)

Mayne, William, ed. (1972), *A Book of Giants*, Puffin, Penguin Books. ("Clever Oonagh" is a favourite story that children find very funny.)

Mosel, Arlene (1968), *Tikki Tikki Tembo*, Henry Holt. (Explains why Chinese parents no longer give their firstborn children long names.)

———(1972), *The Funny Little Woman*, Dutton. (story about a little woman who liked to make rice dumplings and laugh, "Tee-he-he-he". One day she is taken by the wicked oni and forced to make them rice dumplings with a magic paddle. She escapes with the paddle and becomes very rich.)

O'Hare, Colette (1978), *What Do You Feed Your Donkey On? Rhymes from a Belfast Childhood*, Collins. (Collection of Irish songs, chants, rhymes and limericks.)

Phelps, Ethel Johnston, ed. (1978), *Tatterhood and Other Tales*, Feminist Press. (Folktales with role-breaking male and female characters. Brief endnotes to each tale give additional information.)

———(1982), *The Maid of the North: Feminist Folk Tales from Around the World*, Henry Holt.

Riordan, James (1980), *The Three Magic Gifts*, Methuen. (Story about two Russian brothers, one rich and one poor. The rich brother is eventually taught a lesson for being greedy and selfish.)

———(1985), *The Woman in the Moon and Other Tales of Forgotten Heroines*, Dial. (Fourteen folktales from different countries. All show women in unstereotypic roles.)

Robinson, Adjai (1974), *Singing Tales of Africa*, Charles Sintener's Sons. (Seven lively African stories to involve the audience in song. All the stories have a part which can be sung—musical notation is given.)

Ross, Tony (1986), *Foxy Fables*, Dial. (Funny retellings of Aesop fables which will appeal to children's sense of humour.)

Roughsey, Dick (1973), *The Giant Devil-Dingo*, Collins.

Schimmel, Nancy (1987), *Just Enough to Make a Story*, Sisters Choice. (Offers useful advice on selecting and learning stories to tell, and an assortment of stories with full text; excellent bibliography of more good stories.)

Scott, Bill, ed. (1988), *Complete Book of Australian Folklore*, PR Books. (Traditional songs, folktales, poems, 'fillers' and anecdotes which give a strong feeling of Australia's past.)

————(1990), *Many Kinds of Magic*, Viking. (Not-so-familiar folktales from different countries are retold in a manner in keeping with their origins and genre. A very useful collection.)

Seuling, Barbara (1978), *The Teeny Tiny Woman*, Puffin. (Old English ghost story that is not too frightening. Children enjoy the repetition of the words *teeny*, *tiny* throughout the story.)

Shah, Idries (1979), *World Tales*, Harcourt Brace Jovanovich. (Includes "The Riddles", a story which tells how a wood-gatherer's clever daughter saves the kingdom by solving a demon's riddles.)

Spier, Peter, ill. (1977), *The Great Flood*, World's Work Children's Books. (Wordless picture book that lends itself beautifully to oral retelling using the pictures.)

Stewart, M. (1987), *Creation Myths*, ill. Graeme Base, Macmillan. (Retellings of creation myths from many different cultures, which help to show the similarities and diversity of these early explanations for the world and the universe.)

Stobbs, W. (1965), *Jack and the Beanstalk*, Constable.

Stories Round the World (1990), Hodder & Stoughton. (Traditional and contemporary stories which reflect their cultural origins. Stories are arranged according to age level, from young children to teenagers.)

Tashjian, Virginia (1966), *Juba This and Juba That: Story Hour Sketches for Large and Small Groups*, Little, Brown. (Excellent source for games, chants and other activities that could be used in a storytelling program.)

Wolkstein, Diane (1987), *The Magic Orange Tree: And Other Haitian Folktales*, Schocken. (Collection of Haitian tales with notes on the culture and how Wolkstein observed the stories being told. Very good for older children through to adults.)

Zipes, Jack (1986), *Don't Bet on the Prince: Contemporary Feminist Fairy Tales in North America and England*, Routledge, Chapman & Hall.